TO BE A

REDGRAVE

Surviving Amidst the Glamour

By Deirdre Redgrave
and Danaë Brook

THE LINDEN PRESS/SIMON & SCHUSTER

NEW YORK / 1982

Published by The Linden Press/Simon & Schuster
A Simon & Schuster Division of Gulf & Western Corporation
Simon & Schuster Building
Rockefeller Center
1230 Avenue of the Americas
New York, New York 10020
THE LINDEN PRESS / SIMON & SCHUSTER and colophon are trademarks of
Simon & Schuster
Designed by Eve Kirch
Manufactured in the United States of America

1   3   5   7   9   10   8   6   4   2

Library of Congress Cataloging in Publication Data

Redgrave, Deirdre, 1939–
To be a Redgrave.

1. Redgrave, Corin.   2. Redgrave, Deirdre,
1939–   .   3. Redgrave family.   4. Actors—Great
Britain—Biography.   5. Wives—Great Britain—
Biography.   I. Brook, Danaë.   II. Title.
PN2598.R417R4   1982   792'.028'0924   [B]   82-10033
ISBN 0-671-42429-7

Acknowledgments

I have never kept a diary, so I thank the many people who have helped me relive my past—reminding me of good times, and of those more painful. I would also like to mention a few of the many whose emotional and financial support, kindness and generosity have been my mainstay during the writing of this book: First, Mark Colivet; also Maggi Randall, Jo Calthorpe, Patrick and Andrea Hamilton-Hill, Donald and Cynthia Hamilton-Hill, Penny Gordon, Stuart Cornock, Trisha Edwards, Dr. Barrington Cooper, Peter Eyre, Benny Grey, Louise Fitzgerald, Joan Hughes, Earl Green, John "Pleasure" Reilly, Mr. Henry Jones of the National Westminster Bank, Baker Street, Christine and Maurice Barnsley, Mr. A. J. Watts, and finally Jemma and Luke, and Peter, Orion, Liam, and Terence.

I would also like to thank Don Short, our editor, Joni Evans, for having believed in Danaë and myself, and Susan David, her associate. Their hard work and excellent advice have been invaluable.

Most of all, I want to thank Danaë Brook. She has taught me much and has remained, through all the ups and downs of an intimate collaboration, a loving and generous friend.

DEIRDRE REDGRAVE

To my children, Jemma and Luke,
and the memory of my beloved parents,
Edward and Diana

Introduction

Deirdre Redgrave came to me in the Spring of 1980 with the proposition that we write this book. She had left Corin Redgrave four years earlier, when life as the wife of actor-turned-political fanatic became overwhelming. In her stand for independence, she was faced with the predicament of making ends meet while juggling a competitive career and raising their two children, Jemima and Luke.

Corin was now living with Kika Markham, ironically the very actress who had first introduced him to the Worker's Revolutionary Party, and with their baby son. One day a letter arrived addressed to Deirdre's solicitor from Corin's family solicitors stating that not only could he not "make any offer of maintenance" for his children, but that Deirdre was to supply particulars of her own means "as a result of which it may be that we shall advise our client to apply for maintenance against your client."

I was intrigued by the paradox of the Redgrave family, who were known to be controversial and eccentric. What could have happened to make a man as privileged, educated, and talented as Corin Redgrave—far better equipped than most of the male population of England to support his own family—abandon his acting career and even consider that his former wife not only be the sole support of his children but of himself as well? It did not make sense. As it did not make sense that Corin's sister Vanessa, fanatical champion of the proletariat, was still so attached to middle-class values that she left her children with nannies for long stretches of time while she was away, and still shopped at Harrods.

I knew that since the time Deirdre had married Corin she had been besieged by requests for her life story. I also knew that until this moment she had refused. But when her former husband's legal letter put the financial wedge between her and her past, the walls of loyalty collapsed.

Deirdre Redgrave's story is not only a fascinating insight into life with one of the most enigmatic, glamorous, and artistically compelling theatrical families in history, but it is, too, symbolic of the tough realities and sometimes astounding difficulties still encountered by women who have the courage to seek individual growth outside the marriage tradition.

To Be a Redgrave, then, like all good stories, is one of illusion and disillusion, dreams and broken dreams. There is a Royal Family with its fair-haired Prince of Glass and courtiers. And a vulnerable woman reaching first for romance against all emotional odds, then for identity against all social odds, and finally for independence against all financial odds. Whether the ending is happy or not depends entirely upon your point of view—not just on sentimental journeys, but on politics, passion, and the power of the will.

DANAË BROOK

Contents

Photo section follows page 94.

Meeting

He smoked a lot. Disque Bleu, I remember. I thought that was stylish. He drank little. I studied his face as he talked. Rather like Jean-Paul Belmondo. Same mouth. Ice-blue eyes, cold, aloof. I began to sense the isolation behind the air of contempt and wanted to make him relax, feel happy. My fear of him began to melt.

When my friend Jonathan left us alone for a while, I looked at him hard.

"Does making other people feel uncomfortable give you some sort of satisfaction?" I asked. For the first time that evening, he had no easy reply. He looked back at me saying nothing. We just stared at each other, our eyes magnets.

And I knew then that I wanted to break from my way of life, to become part of his. I wanted him to teach me, to like me, to want me, maybe even to love me. I determined that he would.

I was to love him with more intensity for more years than I could ever have imagined possible as I leaned across that table and quietly helped myself to one of his cigarettes. I was raising the curtain on a play that had already begun.

I had heard a great deal about Corin Redgrave before we met. His school friend Jonathan Benson had been my best friend and constant escort for four years. On a black evening in 1962, the streets of London drenched with rain, I went with Jonathan to see Corin Redgrave as Lysander in A *Midsummer Night's Dream.*

I was twenty-two. Jonathan, whom I loved but was not in love with, had taught me a great deal about the arts and dragged me to films and plays and galleries that I never would have discovered without him. We shared a passion for theater, and I looked forward to seeing the play.

It was a new production directed by Tony Richardson, known as a catalyst of style—an original, inventive, daring artist who could be counted upon to surprise you whether you liked it or not. The cast was scooped from the cream of London's young acting talent, including Corin, his younger sister Lynn, Nicol Williamson, Rita Tushingham, Samantha Eggar, Alfred Lynch and David Warner.

The auditorium was already darkened as we slid down into our seats. I held my breath like a child in that magical hushed pause before the curtain goes up. One of my favorite sensations in the world is the moment before the stage appears and I am seduced by the sense of suspended reality in which anything can take place as the force of someone else's imagination bends your own.

I did not know that this sense of wonder, of one's own malleability, is a fertile ground for the seeds of drama which all actors love to sow. If Corin did not know this consciously, certainly he was to use it unconsciously, to the point where I followed him down a path I not only could not see but would find I did not want to follow at all.

At the instant Lysander appeared on stage, I was struck by the sheer force of Corin Redgrave's physical presence. Nothing I knew about the man had prepared me for his brilliant golden aura. Not Jonathan, laughing about boyish escapades or describing respectfully his friend's achievement of the highest honors degree granted at Cambridge, a double first. Not the hundreds of films I had watched his father stride through so elegantly, or the pictures I had seen of his funny, chubby sister Lynn, or the sight of his older sister Vanessa marching with banners for the Campaign for Nuclear Disarmament.

I had not expected him to be such a handsome man. He had eyes so blue they glittered in the lights and a taut lithe grace that made me sit up in my seat and watch only him for the rest of the play.

As I sat in the dark watching the history unfold, I was excited that Jonathan had arranged for us all to meet for dinner. Would Corin be as compelling offstage as on, or would he stamp all over my fantasy once he wore sensible shoes and a pair of trousers?

Halfway through the third act I crept out of the stalls, much to Jonathan's annoyance, and slipped upstairs to the Ladies to repair my makeup, brush my hair and hastily straighten my seams. I looked in the mirror. The face that peered out at me was flushed with excitement. I took out my mascara, wet the brush and spent longer than usual painting my lashes a deeper and darker brown so they framed the brown of my eyes.

"What," I admonished myself, "are you doing this for? You haven't even met the man!"

Jonathan had chosen a restaurant called The Casserole for dinner. It was, depending on your point of view, a busy, colorful meeting place on the King's Road for people who liked to live well and eat cheaply, a veritable gem in the heart of Chelsea— or it was a raucous hodgepodge of opinionated gossips, crazy clothes, careless service and inedible food. Jonathan and I loved it.

The Casserole seemed like a circus ring where every evening a jumble of brilliantly dressed performers would stream into its center. With painters and photographers and models and out-of-work actors and hairdressers and writers and dozens of mysterious eccentrics who lurked on the fringes of the Chelsea scene, there was always the feeling someone was throwing a party. Whether the people we met were successful, hadn't made it, or were on their way down, they had a brave style and a racy flair for living that we enjoyed. To say nothing of the simple, delicious menu, particularly the homemade steak and kidney pie—and, as we were both night birds, the fact that it stayed open later than anywhere else we knew was a bonus.

As we three walked out of the Royal Court Theater and down the King's Road, sheltering under Jonathan's umbrella, it remained to be seen whether Corin Redgrave would like it too.

He had only to put one foot inside the restaurant for me to see that this was not the sort of place he was used to. The expression on his face was wary. In a flash I imagined him dining quietly at his club as he buried his head in a book.

He did not seem to like it any better once we'd been seated at our table, festive with a red tablecloth and a flickering candle, but too small for his long legs. He looked at the chattering table-hoppers with disdain. I could see how all the people I had thought of as dashing rebels and leaders of style looked to him like a tangle of fools.

I remained silent while he and Jonathan discussed theater, politics and philosophy, quoting writers I had never heard of. I could see he was wonderfully intelligent, with an incisive academic mind that had me whirling in confused admiration. The more arrogant and disdainful he was, the more intrigued I became.

Everything I said sounded stupid to me. Everything he said sounded brilliant. He was deliberately ignoring me much of the time, and I was not used to being ignored. Now and then someone would stop to say hello and Corin could barely conceal his contempt for what he had clearly decided were "my sort of friends." Usually it felt good to be greeted by people, to exchange news. This time it was becoming a nightmare.

And yet, and yet, under it all was a current, a feeling between us which lay unacknowledged until our brief exchange of words alone. All through the evening I had had an intuitive feeling that this man was going to mean something special to me, so I, at least, was not surprised when he asked us back to the Redgraves' for a drink, although Jonathan was.

The Redgraves' London home was an impressive apartment in exclusive Knightsbridge, right next door to Harrods, the elegant department store. Corin explained that he spent some of his time there, some staying with his sister Vanessa in Earl's Court. As he fumbled with the key and pushed open the heavy door, it was obvious there was no one else at home. A relief. I didn't want to handle meeting one of the most famous actors in England while my whole body was a cage for butterflies.

"Have a brandy," said Corin, not asking, just handing me one. I didn't drink much, and never spirits, but I agreed. I was floating. It was as though all decisions were out of my hands.

Corin and Jonathan sat down in the living room, talking animatedly about theater, about Richardson's controversial production, about Corin's eccentric family and Jonathan's work as an assistant director. It was theater talk: who was starring in what, who was acting with whom, what production was coming next. I was almost completely excluded. Their jokes were jokes from shared schooldays. They were immersed in each other.

But one thing had changed. At dinner Corin had barely looked at me. Now I could feel his eyes slant away from Jonathan and rest on me. Even if I couldn't see it, I knew, and I had the same feeling that I'd had in the theater when I first saw him. A heightened awareness, apprehension, but mostly excitement.

I was, of course, much too sophisticated to let it show. I wandered through the flat, curious but feigning indifference.

I found the high-ceilinged rooms decorated traditionally, with floor-length curtains and wall-to-wall carpets. Polished antiques were set against curtains of pale yellow and damask. I had been in many such rooms in my life. But what set this one aside from the others was that the walls were covered, end to end, with myriad pictures of Sir Michael in every single performance of his career: *Hamlet* at Elsinore in 1950; *Hamlet* with the Shakespeare Memorial Theater Company in the Soviet Union in 1958;

The Lady Vanishes with Margaret Lockwood; *The Tempest;*
King Lear; The Importance of Being Earnest—to name a few.

Some were paintings. Some were theater bills. Some were
posters or stills from his movies. It was like a portrait gallery of
a hundred different men with one thing in common—piercing
light blue eyes and, whatever the role or disguise, a strong,
distinguished bearing that I had seen that night in his son.

Scripts lay on the coffee table, and programs were scattered
all over the flat, even in the loo. On the mantelpiece in the vast
drawing room dozens of hand-engraved invitations stood like
sentinels. Addressed to Sir Michael or to Sir Michael and Lady
Redgrave, they ranged from invitations to opening nights of
friends and family to receptions at Buckingham Palace.

Corin poured me another brandy without my asking, and went
on talking to Jonathan as I tottered about his home trying to
synthesize what I saw and maintain enough poise to appear comfortable. All the time I felt Corin's eyes on me as though he was
touching me.

I was standing by the window looking out on the dark rain-
swept streets when I heard him get up and walk across to the
grand piano, which, huge and elegant, filled the corner of the
drawing room. He started to play the tough card sharp's song
that Brando sings to Jean Simmons in the film *Guys and Dolls.*

When he reached the line "You're the only one I've ever
wanted to share it with," he looked straight at me. I fell in love.
It was that simple. And that complicated.

Corin and Deirdre

Corin and I were both born in 1939, within six months and sixty miles of each other. I arrived first, at Hartley Grange, a massive estate in Hampshire, to a traditional naval family, whose ancestors (Serlo de Burgh, who came to England with William the Conqueror, and the famous admiral Lord Thomas Graves, who commanded the British Fleet against the French in 1794, among others) had made their mark on the pages of English history. I surprised my mother enormously by arriving in January; I was not expected for at least another month. She said that it was typical of me to effect a premature entry into the world on my terms, and in my time.

Corin was born in a London hospital the following July, as and when expected, to an artistic theatrical family, also adventurers. His grandfather, the flamboyant actor-manager Roy Redgrave, nicknamed "Cock of the North," had toured the world and finally settled in Australia, leaving behind many broken hearts and children. His son Michael was the only one to follow in the family tradition.

Corin was the second child of Michael Redgrave and actress Rachel Kempson. Their daughter Vanessa had been born in January of 1937. A second daughter, Lynn, would arrive in March of 1943.

In those days, battle-torn Britain was producing war babies who would be the rebels of the future. Later we would march against nuclear armament, driven by memories of bombs and battles and the holocaust into which we were hurled in the first excruciating years of our lives.

Because my childhood was so fraught with fear, it became vital to me later to strive to create the kind of safe, secure home for my children that the war had made impossible for me to enjoy when I was young. Awareness of war also pushed me along the road to self-sufficiency, since I quickly realized that there is no true security outside one's own strength. In later years I sought inner knowledge and the power to effect change through love within my family and personal life. Corin and Vanessa, on the other hand, tried to change the world.

My earliest memories are of Hartley Grange, the home of my parents' dearest friends, Audrey and Adrian Stoop, where I spent my first four years. My mother and father had a cottage in Buckinghamshire, where they lived when they were first married. When my mother became pregnant with me, my father did not want her living alone, as he and Adrian were off to protect their country. It seemed a wise arrangement for the two wives to take care of each other in the absence of the men. There were servants at Hartley Grange who could cosset my mother during the months of her pregnancy, and vast vegetable gardens to provide fresh food and nourishment for the unborn baby at a time when most people were hard pressed to find an ounce of butter.

Hartley Grange, my childhood home, was an enormous rambling ivy-covered mansion with sweeping lawns and cedar trees in the garden, creaking corridors and dusty attics. It was even rumored to have a ghost: a perfect place for a little girl to live in a private dream world of princesses and dragons, angels and demons.

The Stoops entertained lavishly. I would creep downstairs and watch guests feasting in the oak-paneled dining room at a table sumptuously laid with silver and crystal, while glittering chandeliers caught the hard gleam of diamonds. I listened fascinated to the adult conversation and learned secrets carefully kept hidden from children in the daytime.

But although life there appeared luxurious and serene, far removed from the bomb-blasted streets of London, it was not removed from the terror of war. Even at Hartley Grange I heard the sirens. Sirens were pure terror. Sirens were streaks of madness in the night. Sirens meant shattered windows, glass breaking inward onto our beds, the blankets cut to ribbons. Sirens meant broken daisy chains, tumbling out of apple trees, panic slicing the tranquillity of gentle English summer afternoons, little girls bundled out of the sunlight and into the musty darkness of "home shelters." Every secure routine was rudely interrupted by the screeching; the peace of breakfasts dappled by morning sunlight was shattered, strawberries dropped from our mouths to our plates in a sudden desperate scramble for the air-raid shelter; the innocence of childhood was crushed by claustrophobic fear.

I remember always the sounds and silences of war: the ominous still before the bombs; the screams of the injured; the smell of antiseptic; the ring of the doorbell, which could bring news, any news—cables from the Ministry opened with trembling fingers, letters from loved ones, sometimes messages sent before the death of the writer.

At Hartley Grange the siren would bring the entire household to a standstill. Formal dinners would end in chaos, parlormaids and guests bumping into each other as, protocol forgotten in the haste for survival, they ran to the shelter. Fortunately for the house guests, the shelter was in the wine cellar, which boasted one of the finest collections of Dom Perignon in the country!

"If we're going to our deaths, we might as well enjoy it," my mother used to say as she picked me up and gave me a swift hug before diving underground.

Not everyone, however, dropped protocol. Old Grandmother

Stoop, an impressive old lady of more than eighty, played her role of matriarch to the hilt, despite the falling shrapnel and the lack of a butler. She was much more concerned with keeping up appearances for the morale of the masses than with dodging death. During one air raid, as my mother was busy rounding everyone up to get into the shelter in time, Grandmother Stoop caused an enormous commotion by moving against the stream. She was trying to get out while everyone else was trying frantically to get in.

"I must get back to the house," she informed my mother, "I've left my false teeth behind, I simply must get them."

"I shouldn't worry about them, my dear," replied my mother, "They're dropping bombs you know, not sandwiches!"

My mother gave me an ingrained, unmalicious sense of the absurdity of life and the human condition. Her dry, stoic sense of humor helped me gain a perspective on the insanities and heartaches of growing up as a war baby, diet confined by rationing, healthy adventure restricted by bomb scares, dreams made nightmares by the constant nagging presence of death.

"Blessed is he who keeps his head when all around are losing theirs," she would say. She always kept her head, and her wryly amused attitude toward life.

One Christmas, my mother, desperately trying to normalize the holiday season, took me to see the Pantomime of Snow White in London. Parts of London had been reduced to rubble during some of the heaviest bombing. Attacks that demolished whole chunks of the beautiful city and its communities came out of the sky like battering rams.

We found our way to the theater, and as we found our seats I clutched her hand in great excitement. The lights dimmed, the orchestra started to play, and I was lost in a dream world. Living in fantasy and imagination had become as real to me as cleaning my teeth. The theater spun its magic and I was caught in its spell.

Suddenly, shrieking through the auditorium came the siren wails like demons on the wind. Children's screams of fear rose to

meet them. A cacophony of terror. The entire audience jumped
to its feet as one and ran for the exits. We were sucked into the
nearest subway with hundreds of people, old and young, big and
small, jostled against bodies sweaty with dread.

Snow White and the Seven Dwarfs jumped off the stage as we
ran for shelter and now moved among the children in the crowd,
offering what comfort they could. The fantasy was smashed forever. Never again would pantomime seem real. I was one minute
wrapped in a fairy tale, reveling in the fantasy evil of the wicked
stepmother, and the next minute plunged into real fear. Nothing
made sense. The dividing line between fact and fiction became
completely blurred. Even now, the wail of a police car fills me
with dread.

Eventually, to escape the bombing, like most English children
I became an evacuee. At the age of four, I was sent to a boarding
school farther away from the battle zone while my mother went
to London to do her bit for the war effort, running a hotel in
Wimpole Street for American officers on leave from their regi-
ments.

The two eldest Redgrave children were also evacuated from
the large house in Chiswick where Rachel and Michael lived, to
another large house in the country. In this Victorian mansion in
Herefordshire Vanessa and Corin were raised in comparative
peace and according to the standard of living to which they were
accustomed.

Vanessa was to say later that she was brought up in such a
way that she would probably have become a conservative had
the romance of the left not tugged at her heartstrings. "I believed in king and country, the Empire, the Church of England
and Churchill," she said of her early life.

Surrounded by books, animals and the peace of country living,
the children were protected from the harsher realities of war.
Rachel and Michael continued to act. Michael went into the Navy
as an ordinary seaman in July 1941, but was out again in just
over a year.

The Redgrave children led as normal a life as is ever possible in war. But while they played happily in attic nurseries, I, aged four, separated from both my parents, was unable to sleep because of the sound of children even younger than I crying for their parents and homes. My memories of that time are etched in pain; Corin's always seemed to me to be blurred by the cushioning a secure childhood gives, war or no war.

Vanessa and Corin grew very close during their war years. They had no friends in Herefordshire and relied almost exclusively on each other for company. Most of all they enjoyed play-acting with each other. Out of their imaginations they created magic worlds for themselves. They became princes and princesses, pirates, magicians, with little Lynn too young to be anything but their pet dog. Their isolation forged an indestructible bond.

Lynn has always been a little on the outside of Vanessa and Corin's charmed relationship, perhaps because she was too young to participate in those special years. Even to this day she stands outside the tight bond that ties Vanessa and Corin. Vanessa and Corin complement one another perfectly—Corin the intellect, Vanessa the romantic; Corin the teacher, Vanessa the pupil; Vanessa the magnetic, Corin the competitor. Both tall, blond, handsome, with charismatic presence and flashing blue eyes. Sometimes when you see them together, you feel that neither has any real room in their lives for anyone else. Vanessa once said to me, "I will never find for myself a man like Corin."

For eight years I was raised as an only child. My brothers Patrick and Robert were not born until after the war, when my parents had settled peacefully on the island of Malta, where my father had taken a civilian job as a director of Rediffusion, the broadcasting company. My father was a distinguished sportsman. He excelled at tennis and cricket, and played rugger for the Royal Navy and the Harlequins, England's most famous amateur team. Perhaps to please him I became a tomboy, competing fiercely on the tennis court, winning prizes at riding, water skiing and scuba diving.

As masculine as my family balance was, Corin's childhood, on the other hand, was spent surrounded by women—nannies, maids and sisters. I often felt he became aloof, something of a recluse, because he needed to protect his male identity in this household of women. He put up barriers that took many years to break through.

As his parents were away so much of the time, Corin fell into a paternal role with both his sisters. He was the man of the household, almost a substitute father, an attitude so ingrained that it exists even to this day.

Michael was home so seldom that Corin had no strong male archetype on which to model himself. On the rare occasions that Michael was not away working, if Corin wanted to talk to his father, he often found Michael closeted in his study, reading or preparing a new script. Rashly made promises of new bicycles or fishing rods wound the boy up with excitement until the day of presentation dawned and his parents had forgotten the promise, forgotten the importance of the gift to their son. It was not intentional, just thoughtless, but I know it happened often enough to hurt.

So Corin became guarded. I am not sure if he has ever completely dropped that guard. He also learned much of the ways and wiles of headstrong women, and was to tell me how exasperating it was to live with women and how he found them "totally impossible creatures." It was the lack of logic which frustrated him most I think and the fear of the superficiality of girls' emotions. So as he grew older, he grew more and more cerebral, clinging to facts he could learn from books.

I on the other hand was becoming less guarded in my new environment. I was blossoming in the Mediterranean sun. The years of fear had melted into the shadowy past and I now had friends who wouldn't disappear in the next air raid. I had a family and security and I was happy. But when I was twelve my parents arranged for me to be sent to a boarding school in France, strictly in keeping with the English tradition of rearing their young as far away from the soft comforts of home as possible. It seemed like complete rejection. I felt consigned like a package to the fate of the traditional schoolgirl. It meant five years of convents, tuck boxes, gray socks, no contact with boys, no privacy, morning chapel, and whispering dormitory nights—the kind of fate few mothers today would dare impose on their daughters.

As time went by I tried to understand and accept that my parents had made the choice for me that they thought best. As much as any child of twelve can, I sensed that, rather than rejecting me, they actually believed it was good for young girls to live in the cloistered atmosphere of the convent, with only other girls or austere nuns for company.

I am sure now that they felt I needed discipline. Running barefoot on the beaches of Malta was not a fitting upbringing for a young woman whose future was to be first that of a well-bred debutante, performing exquisitely the mannered dance of The Season, and then, having snared a suitable husband, to follow all the young colonial matrons into comfortable marriage to comfortable men with comfortable incomes.

My very conventional parents realized that a good Roman Catholic convent would provide me with a suitable education for my well-planned destiny. They never knew of my homesickness, the wave of nostalgia which engulfed me every time I had to leave my wondrous amber island for the hard beds of our dark dormitories.

Of course, most of us transferred our affection to our teachers. In my case, however, religion, the very fabric of convent life, became my mainstay and my emotional salvation. As my parents became ever more shadowy figures throughout my adolescence, the pomp and ceremony of organized religion gave me a feeling of security in a constantly shifting world, a faith I carried with me as I was moved from one school to another with my parents' changing ideas of education.

I said Mass, took Communion every morning, sang hymns and inhaled incense, believing that someone somewhere was looking after me, however naughty I might be, and this was tremendously reassuring. The feeling of displacement and insecurity that had started in the war was gradually soothed by the idea that God and the Church would always be there for me to lean on.

Paradoxically, as children will, I fought the very people who led me to religion. I fought "Authority." Delighting in ritual but angered by regulations, I became known as a "troublemaker." My daily life in the convent was bound not only by high brick walls but also by so many rules and regulations (which I broke) and silences, punishments and penances (which I endured). As much as I desperately wanted to believe in something, anything, I violently rebelled against the seemingly mindless discipline by which adults seek to subdue the spirit of the young.

Perhaps my rebelliousness was because of an emotional lack— there was no one to answer the questions arising from the adolescent curiosity about love and sex. The nuns talked about marriage, but they didn't talk about sex. It was not done. It was not "nice." Forbidden music—the pop music of the radio, not the classical concerts we were forced to listen to—excited me with its lyrics boldly celebrating love and "kisses of fire." The little wireless hidden under my bed transmitted to me the first ideas of another way of life. For years since, music has been one of the strongest symbols of rebellion in my life.

Perhaps it was the system and those who enforced it that made me a rebellious child. The uniforms. The rules. There was no room for originality. As a child I was thoroughly conditioned to fear, and therefore to obey, authority in all its many guises. My individual spirit rebelled, but it had nowhere to go. No one to confide in. I was always and immediately made to feel guilty for questioning the status quo. My conditioning required me to conform to other people's ideas of what life was all about, although my heart insisted on independence.

I believed—as the nuns were to say so frequently that it became like a monotonous chant—"A woman has two choices in life —to be a good wife and mother or to take the veil."

So enamored was I of religion that at one point I even considered becoming a nun. But I did not "have a vocation." I had not "seen a vision which led me to Our Savior." Therefore I could not join the nuns and serve Him for the rest of my life.

What did that mean? Simply that to be good, to be worthy of my school, my parents and my country, I should become a good wife and mother. And as soon as possible.

Corin and his sisters, on the other hand, were born to the avant-garde. They were not only allowed freedom to express themselves, they were expected to do so. Their spirits were encouraged, nudged, along the road to independence early. It was not until I left school, had lived away from my parents in the heart of London and had single-handedly rejected the maps drawn up for my future that I experienced a freedom anywhere near theirs.

All three Redgrave children went to day schools. Their family life had a much broader, more sophisticated base than mine. Their dinner-table conversations were about art and philosophy and politics. When I was home, ours revolved around sport and social gossip.

While Corin's family were discussing Shakespeare and his ideas of murder, incest and magic, I was taught to believe that no such realities existed. The most important things my parents discussed with me were the next tennis party, the most suitable escort, and where I should shop for my school wardrobe.

When Corin and I first met he had just graduated from King's College, Cambridge, with that double first in English mentioned earlier. He was already moderately interested in left-wing politics, not surprisingly, since he came from the same college as two of the most famous and controversial double agents in British political history—Burgess and Maclean, two apparently patriotic Englishmen who defected to Russia amidst one of the greatest British scandals of this century.

During the time Corin was at Cambridge he was extremely studious. When others were attending May balls, punting on the River Cam, dating debutantes and quaffing champagne, Corin was studying. The only time he took off from his pursuit of excellence, as his father described it, was when he was acting in, or directing, student productions.

He was a gifted pianist and had every intention of becoming a serious musician, writer, actor or director. Anyway, a serious *something*. It was part of his background and part of his training. He came from very serious people. The Redgrave children were always striving to live up to Sir Michael's patrician image and daunting theatrical accomplishments.

"The fact that we were always surrounded by successful, ambitious people made all of us ambitious ourselves," Corin told me. "My parents' closest friends included Laurence Olivier, Vivien Leigh, Sir John and Lady Mills, Ralph Richardson and Yvonne Mitchell. All of them had achieved great artistic and commercial success. They were our models. We couldn't escape the dream of perfection."

Their circle also included people such as Dame Peggy Ashcroft, George Devine (the man responsible for starting the Royal Court Theater), and actress Rosalie Crutchley. Since early childhood, achievement, preferably theatrical or intellectual, was a priority instilled within each of the Redgrave children.

Sir Michael was acclaimed throughout the world as a brilliant actor, and the children had to learn to live with that. There was a sense of latent competition in the family which I could always sense, but which Corin always denied.

Although Sir Michael's intellectual success was not as stunning as Corin's, it is quite possible that Corin was spurred on by the fact that his father had taught at Cranleigh, a small, elite public school in the depths of the English countryside, before going on into repertory.

Corin's mother, Rachel Kempson, was considered a great beauty. Unlike my own mother, who pursued only the career of wife and mother after her stint of war work, Rachel was also an actress of formidable ability in her own right.

Unusual as it was in those days, Rachel completely rejected her conventional background in favor of the theater. She met and married Michael Redgrave in 1934, when they were both appearing with the Liverpool Repertory Theater Company. It seems she fell madly in love with her handsome costar, and for her it was a lifelong commitment.

Years later she would tell me about it, and we would laugh together as we discovered how similar our backgrounds were. Rachel was the daughter of the Captain (headmaster) of Dartmouth College, the school where young officers of the British Navy were honed to the perfection of discipline, health and intelligence needed for their command of His Majesty's fleet.

Although, like me, she went to a convent boarding school, Rachel was the toast of the Dartmouth cadets whenever she was at home. According to my father's naval friends, she broke many a young heart, and at the end-of-term balls, the young men drew lots to see who would dance with her.

Vanessa bears a striking facial resemblance to her mother, but somehow lacks her femininity, perhaps because Vanessa is so much taller. Vanessa's first love was ballet—a training that would stand her in good stead for her magnificent performance as Isadora Duncan—but she grew too tall for that. So when she left Queen's Gate girls' school, she went straight to the Central School of Speech and Drama, where she strove to follow in her father's footsteps.

Corin, on the other hand, sort of drifted into acting. First and foremost an academic, he directed as much as acted while at Cambridge, and first went to the Royal Court as assistant director to Tony Richardson, then newly married to Vanessa.

Corin had no burning ambition to be an actor; in fact I don't believe he even thought about acting seriously until he was cast as the pilot officer in Arnold Wesker's *Chips with Everything*, just before we were married. It ran for eighteen months in London's West End, and six on Broadway.

Lynn had no great ambition to act either. Although they played their childhood games to the hilt, Lynn quite happy to fall on all fours as the pet dog of her royal family, the stage did not attract her until many years later.

As Corin grew older he grew more and more cerebral, clinging to facts he could read from books more than the emotional experiences of art. How ironic that what Corin learned from Marx, I learned from rock and roll: a revolutionary way of living. Where academic achievement was almost meaningless to me, it became all-important to him. Life at Cambridge was austere because he unhesitatingly chose the way of the intellectual and the esthete, true to the tradition of his distinguished college.

Corin was friendly with a small elite circle of theatrical people who were soon to rise to individual stardom. Their social commitment to the theater lured him, so he moved in and out of their "scene" with the kind of ease he had developed at Westminster School, where he not only acted but became junior fencing champion of the U.K. It was during this time that he became close to people who were to be part of the experimental arts world at King's College—people who were to remain friends all his life, such as Peter Cook, David Frost, Margaret Drabble, Clive Swift and Ian McKellen. Although there were several Cambridge productions in which he acted or directed or wrote (his favorite aspect of the theater always seemed to be directing), it was due only to Tony Richardson's persuasion that he was actually appearing in that production of *A Midsummer Night's Dream* at the time we met.

It was to strike me later that he had a more than physical similarity to my father. Both were tall, blond, blue-eyed, athletic. But more important, they had an almost identical puritan streak which I found exasperating. Being wildly irresponsible, scatty, forgetful, untidy and liberal in my thinking, I would find myself constantly brought up short by the authoritarianism in them both.

My father's sense of integrity was born at home, honed by his family, the Navy and inbred principles of Tory superiority. He was, and felt he always should be, a pillar of the Establishment.

Corin's philosophies, although formed in the cool corridors of King's College and shaped by avid study and the constant, virtually addictive, reading of books, seemed to emerge as almost the same. Honor, virtue, truth, consideration, all were essential to daily life. Unfortunately that also meant always making your bed, never telling white lies, never ducking authority to have fun.

My father's conventional sense of honor took the form of "doing what is right," which to him meant doing one's duty to king and country.

To Corin, honor has always been more a question of doing what is right according to one's individual conscience.

As far as anyone had to date, Corin filled the bill of romantic suitor for me. He could play the knight errant without effort, and I am a hopeless romantic. Not only was he clearly destined to be famous, which was thrilling for a young girl, however sophisticated she might feel, but he was handsome and clever. He cut a distinguished figure wherever he went. His wit was razor sharp, and he could always make me laugh. I repeatedly felt a shiver of pride when I went out with him and people turned to stare.

I wanted him. Not because he was an eligible bachelor like the wet and weak-chinned minor members of the English aristocracy thrust hopelessly in my direction by my parents. No, I wanted him because he radiated the sure confidence of a man aware of his own power. I found it irresistible from the start.

Of course there were more things to life, more things I found I wanted from a man, from a relationship. But I was still young, and extremely naive. My goals in life were far from clear.

Somehow Corin seemed to bring me closer to the undefined dream of "perfect mate" so relentlessly instilled by school and society.

By the time I met him I was tired of dating acceptable boring young "gentlemen" with excellent pedigrees and no spines. And I was tired of fighting my parents' idea of suitable suitors by dragging home snarling bikers with greased hair and "absolutely no manners."

I had felt a sneaky glow of triumph every time I tempted and teased some unruly boyfriend into the stilted atmosphere of my parents' disapproving company. Remembering passionate song lyrics, I was thrilled to act out the role of temptress. But I really agreed with my parents' assessments. Black leather *was* better on the road, where the roar of Harley-Davidsons drowned out the monosyllabic grunts of my cherished outlaws, than in the house.

In Corin I found a white knight to fit my fairest fantasies. Although my straitlaced parents enjoyed going to plays, they looked somewhat askance upon the world of the theater, regarding most actors about as stable as gypsies, but they took to Corin personally. Corin was a sportsman, junior fencing champion of Great Britain no less, and that my athletic father could certainly relate to. He was light and bright and full of grace, and besides, his father was actually a Knight of the British Empire, and that was more than acceptable to both my parents.

He offered me a whole new unknown world. He opened the door to the excitement of glamour, fame, success and art. He showed me that elusive freedom I had never had but always craved, he beguiled me with the promise of true love and that elusive security I had never had but always craved.

How could I know he was only mortal? I saw him as a god. How could they all, my teachers, my parents, my peers, do anything but approve? They could respect him for all their various reasons. But best of all, so could I.

"Until I die," I thought then. "Until I die." Nobody told me how shortsighted I was. That I found out for myself.

3

Courtship

Jonathan, Corin and I became a permanent threesome. We went to the movies and to theaters, to dinners in cheap Chelsea restaurants and funky little places in Soho, which Corin grew to like, where we'd eat Chinese, Indian or Italian food, according to mood and pocket. He also began to share our old enthusiasm for dinner and gambling at the White City dog track. We would sit behind the glass panels which separated the diners from the dogs, enjoy a delicious meal, and hand our bets to runners, who would place them for us with nearby bookmakers.

"I won't go on form," I used to say to Corin and Jonathan. "I don't understand all that stuff about pedigree and I can't be bothered to read it."

Of course Jonathan, a dyed-in-the-wool gambler who always followed form whether for dogs or horses, was appalled. He used to slough off my choices, saying I'd never win, and then be utterly cowed when my dog, chosen for the sake of its name, came galloping in to win.

"If it's called Rita Hayworth," I told Corin, "I'll back it even if it's only got three legs!"

"I'm following Jonathan," he said. "I like winning."

In the end I would win more often than they did, and it caused such rows when Jonathan's dogs lost that he stopped telling Corin which one he was going to back.

It was my first intimation of Corin's inability to lose gracefully. He could never have been described as a good sport, a quality that my family revered with awe. However, I found something rather endearing about it. There is a quality of totally committed earnestness one finds in people who are bad sports that exhibits the kind of intensity few people dare express.

Unhappily it often resulted in chess and Scrabble boards flying across the room, and I got used to all the strings on his tennis racquet snapping about three times a summer.

At this time I was sharing a flat close to Sloane Square with two girlfriends. One was a model, the other was trying to break into films. Our small flat in a small terraced Regency house off a small street in Chelsea was not the height of luxury, but we enjoyed it. We lived in the chaos bred by three irresponsible, irrepressible girls at large in London.

I couldn't take a bath without being hit in the eye with a wet stocking. The telephone could not ring without three pairs of eager hands reaching for the receiver. But it was fun to be away from home, fun to share. And for me, now, the best part of it all was that the flat was so near Corin's theater. Almost every day my errands "accidentally" coincided with Corin's trips to and from the Royal Court, he with stage notes under his arm, I with a shopping bag over mine.

"Running into" Corin was a great excuse for us to go out and have a drink or a meal, or catch a movie. These were times of tentative secrecy. Jonathan was best friend to both of us and didn't know of our deepening relationship. No one else knew we were meeting. This sense of cloak and dagger added excitement to a friendship already full of undercurrents.

After six weeks of such meetings, there was still no physical contact between us, no touching, no kissing. We were both too fond of Jonathan. We could not bear to hurt him, and that stopped us from admitting to the fact that we were violently attracted to one another. It would have seemed like a betrayal of our best friend, and against our most basic code of ethics, although I think that in fact we were really too scared to talk about it. It was like a dance. A dance of evasion. Never quite touching. Never quite losing touch.

I decided that even if my schooling had better prepared me for arranging flowers in a country mansion than for providing literary or intellectual challenge to an intelligent man, I would educate myself to match Corin's bank of knowledge.

I would go by myself to see films I felt would interest him so I'd have something to talk about with him. My girlfriends caught me circling obscure French and Swedish films in the evening paper; they giggled at me as I pored over literary reviews, new books and theater critics' columns and switched on the television to listen to the political debates.

They were amazed. They knew that the only art or media forms that had interested me so far were movies such as *The Wild One* and *On the Waterfront*. And any kind of popular music, from the blues through jazz to what was soon to be known as rock and roll.

When I left school at seventeen, my parents, now living once again in London, had made a valiant effort to present me to London society by means of the debutante Season. But it had not really worked. I dodged the string of dates to cocktail parties, tea parties, lunch parties and balls as often and as completely as I could. I failed to land an eligible husband because I not only failed to look for one, I failed to respond to those who looked at me.

When my mother and father returned to their home in Malta and to safer, more predictable ways, my mother only agreed to leave me alone in London on the understanding that I would take a secretarial course. Since I had no wish to be dependent on them, I agreed. I had little choice. The only job opportunities for women were as shopgirls, waitresses, secretaries and starlets. For girls to earn money then in any other way was almost impossible.

If I could type, I could at least find a job in an office, and this I did. It simply did not occur to me to try to carve out a career for myself. I felt lucky to walk away each week with the kind of pittance which would just about pay my rent and keep me in makeup. The job itself was excruciatingly boring, but I never thought that it could be any other way. This job was to fill in the time until I got married and had a man to support me, or so I was told.

So I worked as a secretary to a series of faceless men who did little but dictate tedious business letters, expect me to run their personal lives, and not mind when they pinched my bottom as I bent over their steel filing cabinets.

Occasionally I picked up some modeling jobs because I was, fortunately, photogenic. Modeling brought in a little extra money, but had limited appeal. In the late fifties, early sixties, top models were expected to be clotheshorses. Without exception, the stars of the high-fashion world were tall, bone-thin, and glassy-eyed—truly not my style. Perhaps later, when the slashed miniskirts and free-flying hair of the mid-sixties dropped like a bomb on fashion and models began to look like real people, I might have been more suited and more interested.

While I was nineteen and struggling to find some kind of identity, some possible direction for myself that would not mean either leaning on my parents or continually searching for a man, it seemed as though I faced stone walls at every turn.

The nearest I got to any real rebellion was when my best friend Penny and I ducked the debutante's rounds and succumbed to the lure of the underbelly of London's music life. Together we had roamed the funky basements and dirty streets of Soho looking for excitement.

Penny and I started exploring music clubs when we were supposed to be at cocktail parties. Penny's mother would insist that we dress up and she would drive us to things like Wimbledon or the Eton and Harrow Match and we'd pretend to go in, and then we'd run away!

When I sat and told Corin about our adventures over cups of

foaming cappuccino he would laugh and urge me to continue. He was fascinated both by my convent-colonial background, so different from his, and by my daring excursions into a world he knew nothing about.

I told Corin how, bored to death with all the posing and manners and games of bourgeois life, I had begun sneaking off to Cy Laurie's jazz club, tucked away in a little mews off Wardour Street, where you could smell the sweat of panting bodies limp from dancing, and the language and clothes fairly cried out that anarchy and change were brewing.

As I paid my few shillings and descended the steps into the huge filthy basement, the atmosphere was electrifying. I described to Corin how we wore black stockings, low-heeled T-bar shoes, circular skirts that whirled while we were dancing, or else skintight ones with huge, baggy sweaters that hung almost to the knees. "Lots of mascara and white lipstick," I added. "We were dazzled by all the art students and artists."

It was the first place I'd been to where one's background was irrelevant. Only the love of music was important. I met people with views, opinions and interests that were exciting and new and freeing for me. I needed to belong to this, the first environment which had spoken to me. Perhaps the blues echoed the first lonely years of my life and somehow made them more bearable.

I told Corin how one memorable summer day I had actually seen Louis Armstrong. As I was wandering in the ruins of the Colosseum in Rome, awestruck with the history of the site, I heard fragments of the blues wafting round that tragic place, harmonizing softly with the ancient spirits. I was too shy to talk to him, but the memory of that sight and that sound has never left me.

Eventually "trad jazz," as it was called, became a fashion, like so much else, before it could really become a revolutionary force. The people who played it were packaged and sold. Its soul was trivialized, its badges commercialized. Penny and I moved on— to rock and roll.

When we did our sneaking this time, it was to coffee bars where bikers hung out and played jukebox music by Gene Vincent and Eddie Cochran. This was rougher stuff. These were tough young men in leather jackets looking like Brando and Dean, scary monsters in ducktails with surly frowns and grease on their hair. These were frightening, these were men; the ones we had left behind in their dinner jackets at the ball were boys.

Penny and I would arrive at Piccadilly Circus, head for the Ladies, bouff out our hair and paint on as much mascara with spit as we possibly could, and change into black stockings and stiletto-heeled shoes. When our lashes were almost glued together, we'd slouch our way into the nearest coffee bar. We couldn't look like that at home—we didn't yet have the courage to parade our new-found identities in front of our parents.

Corin listened, fascinated, as I related my teenage secrets.

Very often we went to a seedy little dump called the Two Eyes. It served bacon and eggs and greasy chips, cold tea in cracked mugs, had ghost-green strip lighting that made everyone look sick, and occasionally sported an itinerant musician who'd pick up his instrument and jam for a few quid and some attention from the girls.

Corin laughed. It was another world to him. He had been buried in books while I was learning from the streets.

At the Two Eyes, Penny and I met Tommy Steele. He was one of England's first real rock and rollers. Later he hung up his blue suede shoes and became family fodder, turning his talents to corny musicals and boring ballads, but then he was an East End ruffian. Another friend was Terry Nelhams. He had a group called The Worried Men, which played skiffle, a frantic, jazz-rooted music, the main rattling gurgle of which came from pounding the washboard. Terry Nelhams didn't stick it out for long. He changed his name to Adam Faith and, like Tommy, joined the mainstream. Mickey and Alex Most sang as the Most Brothers. Mickey is now a highly successful record producer.

Penny and I were their official "screamers," I told Corin. It meant that we had to go to the concerts and scream our support for our particular band. It was like being a groupie but you didn't have to go to bed with the musicians. At least, that is what we thought! Every so often we would find ourselves in tricky situations.

It was one thing to slouch around Soho looking as though you knew what was what, but quite another thing to have to prove it. I remembered only too well the threatening reality of the pushing, insistent hands, the smell of whiskey breath and the snarling angry street language, and was glad now of Corin's comforting presence.

For a man so wrapped up in books, rock music opened new areas of feeling, new loyalties and understanding, and gave Corin an unexpected alignment with people of his own generation who had led less privileged lives, people whom he was really only in touch with through the work that he and his sister Vanessa were doing with the Campaign for Nuclear Disarmament.

"You're always so serious!" I chastised. "Too serious."

So I took him to the new clubs that were blossoming, Ronnie Scott's, or the Flamingo, where Georgie Fame and Alexis Korner played all night and people took speed pills called "purple hearts" and raved till morning took the night away.

Corin went to music shops and spent hours listening to the latest records while I was watching an Ingmar Bergman movie alone in some classic cinema, so that I could later discuss it with him! We were both unconsciously turning each other's lives around.

In the dark basements of the clubs to which I took Corin, the pungent smell of marijuana seeped into everything, distinguishing my haunts from the clubs he knew. I had already started to smoke dope at that time, but Corin wouldn't try it, not until later, when the atmosphere of the sixties' drug culture encouraged many people to experiment with psychedelics, including my husband and his sister Vanessa.

But in those early days it was I who took the first tentative puffs on a marijuana joint, and Corin (who later took LSD whereas I never would) was the one who was turning it down.

"Don't need it," was his brief assessment of the situation, reaching, nevertheless, for his glass of wine.

"But it's fun," I pointed out mildly.

Fun was not a concept that particularly appealed to Corin. He would look at me askance as I laughed my way through a movie, chattered my way through a conversation or danced my way through a record.

Still, this apparent contradiction in our personalities didn't strike me as important. We were learning about each other, and our differences were intriguing. There were similarities too. Although the books he preferred were too dry and analytical for me (I opted for Victorian novels), we found we actually liked the same films. And we both liked French food, good wine and walking in cemeteries—Corin because he liked to walk, but not in step with heavy traffic, I because I was still spellbound in the presence of a church or any token of the Christian religion. But although we would walk together through churchyards, he would almost never come inside a church with me.

As we grew to know each other, we grew to like each other and to want to see each other more and more. It became a habit to meet at the stage door after his performance and slip away somewhere quietly for dinner. My flat was too crowded and chaotic for Corin. We rarely went to his house because he seemed to have a curiously distant relationship with his parents. Lady Redgrave spent a great deal of her time at their beautiful little country house, near the ancient village of Odiham, in Hampshire. Corin went there sometimes on Saturdays, partly to see Vanessa, as she was working at Stratford and could only get away from the theater late on Saturday night to have Sunday off. He spoke affectionately of his mother, however, and though she was seldom in London, spoke to her regularly on the telephone. Sir Michael and Corin appeared to have very little contact. Later I discovered they hardly even talked, but would write notes if they wanted to communicate. I was quite shocked, but again, it didn't

seem significant at the time. I did not really know what consti-
tuted "normal" family life.

At this early stage of our relationship what mattered was
being together—in cinemas or bistros. The sexual magnetism
between us built up and up. Frustration added an edge of its
own mystery to heighten our senses. Time together was taken
from the teeth of other commitments, other people. We felt it
was rare and precious and we tried to handle our newfound happiness with delicacy.

It was becoming quite a problem to know what to say to Jonathan. He still played a large part in the lives of both of us. Even
though ours had never been, for me, anything but a platonic
relationship and I had never led him to believe otherwise, I was
beginning to feel uncomfortable with a situation in which I felt I
was less than honest. I was acutely aware of the fact that it had
been Jonathan, who I knew loved me dearly though I had never
reciprocated that love, who had introduced me to his best friend
Corin.

Not being brave enough to do otherwise, I engineered a fight
with Jonathan and told him I wasn't going to see him for two
months. I really needed the space to think out what I felt about
Corin.

But when Corin and I were no longer able to hide the intensity
of our emotions, Corin arranged to see Jonathan. Later that
evening I sat down and took Jonathan's hand and told him Corin
and I had fallen in love.

Jonathan was at first overwhelmed and then furious.

"The worst part is that you haven't told me the truth," he said,
shocked. "I love you, Dee. I thought you knew that." He turned
to Corin. "I thought *you* knew that, you two-timing bastard."

It was a year before he would speak to either of us again.
Corin was upset, but not dreadfully. "He'll get over it." He
shrugged it off, not wanting to probe deeper. "I've known J. a
long time. We'll always be friends."

But I wanted everyone to be happy, everything to be rosy. I
was saddened by Jonathan's reaction and wished he could be

happy for us, for this miraculous experience of being "in love" we were having. But Jonathan's specter was soon dismissed. Swept along by the selfishness of young love, I found it hard to think further than the next meeting with Corin.

4

Meeting the Family

Corin and I had known each other about six weeks when he decided it was time for us to have some time alone. It was spring. In London the parks were covered with violet sheets of early flowers, and the trees were beginning to sprout green buds on the cold black branches of winter.

The Redgraves would gather in their Hampshire cottage every weekend. It was a focal point for all of them, and by now Corin was spending so much time with me that Rachel, and even Vanessa—then newly in love with Tony Richardson, without much time left over for anyone else—were beginning to ask where he kept disappearing to all the time and why he wasn't attending the family gatherings as usual.

One night Corin invited me to dinner at a nightclub. To impress him I borrowed a stunning green satin suit from my friend and flatmate, actress Gloria Kindersley. I wore my hair combed straight back, black-seamed stockings, and the fashionable heavy makeup of the day, including false eyelashes and white lipstick.

For dim lights and holding hands under the table, it was perfect. In fact, I was the height of fashion. Corin was bewitched.

We danced the twist until the early hours and emerged exhausted into the dawn. Then Corin insisted that instead of returning to my London flat I should go down with him to his parents' cottage.

"It's so lovely there, Dee," he said, and his skin was warm as he touched me. We had been dancing for hours. The strength to resist him had ebbed long ago, early in the evening, before he held me.

"There won't be anyone there," he whispered. "I want to be alone with you. We're never alone. We don't have to make love, if that's what you're afraid of, we can just spend some time together in peace. Let's be really alone. Nightclubs are crowded with people. So are cafés and restaurants and jazz clubs and other people's flats. Please, Dee, please."

He has a beautiful resonant voice. It's one of the most seductive things about him. His eyes too. They reflect the light as only blue eyes can, and they were mesmerizing. I remember thinking they were like his father's eyes. Dominant. I remember trying to resist them as we walked toward the car, and worrying about his parents' being there if we did go.

"What will they think?" I asked him. "What will they think of me if I suddenly turn up with you out of the blue like this?"

"They won't be there," he insisted. "There's no one there. It will be just us. And it's my home. It's beautiful. You'll love it."

"I don't want to meet your parents that way," I objected. And what I meant was I didn't want them to think I was a "loose woman," as my mother would have put it. I knew they wouldn't have approved of improper liaisons. And I knew ours was about to become improper. My convent morality was fighting my rebellious nature, as usual. Corin could see that the rebel would win if he could just push the right button.

"They won't be there," he said again. "There'll be no one there. And when my family does meet you they'll love you as much as I do."

"But I'm confused, Corin," I said miserably. Until now we could not have made love. There was nowhere to go. I shared a flat. He lived with his parents. The decision was out of my hands, and I was glad for that. Now I had to face reality, and I wasn't glad.

This confusion about my own moral standards tore me apart. I really wanted to be with him but was afraid. Nameless fears of losing him if it were all too easy, guilt instilled by Catholicism, of what my mother would think and his mother would think and the whole world would think.

But I let him lead me to his smart red, borrowed Thunderbird convertible, let him open the door and help me inside, and once I was in there, imprisoned, I knew I was on my way. Corin was at the wheel, literally and metaphorically. I was in his hands.

We drove through the quiet countryside hardly speaking. I just kept thinking how beautiful everything looked. As though freshly washed, while the light slowly shredded the dark like a pale exquisite veil across the sky and the sun began to rise. We reached Odiham village, huddled and ancient like something from an old postcard, a dream of Olde England. The Redgraves' cottage was ravishing—my ideal of a country cottage, centuries old, covered in climbing roses and honeysuckle with here and there the delicate lilac of a clematis.

"How wonderful," I said to Corin, awestruck. "How perfect. It's like a dream house. Something from a fairy story."

Corin said nothing. Just smiled that slow sweet smile of his and took me by the hand to lead me through the gate and across the lawn. Still silent, we walked hand in hand and crossed the wooden bridge that arched over a small ornamental lake and led to a studio quite separate from the main house.

"This is my father's studio," he told me. "He likes to be with the family but he also guards his privacy. He's had his own place since we bought the house ten years ago."

He opened the door quietly. It was a little cottage, really, separate from the main house, compact, self-contained and very old. There was a huge fireplace in the living room, the inevitable theatrical posters on the wall. The Redgraves, I couldn't help thinking, seemed to decorate their homes with their work. All on one level was a pretty drawing room, a tiny bathroom and a comfortable bedroom overlooking the lake.

It was nearly dawn and the birds were just beginning to stir and call out to each other. Mist rose like curling licks of steam from the lake. I watched Corin's long-fingered, elegant hands as he poured brandy for us and thought how beautiful they were.

But even though I was here, alone with him at last, I was still vacillating about whether or not I should sleep with him.

The only other love relationship I had had was with a young Maltese army officer. He was barely twenty, I was sixteen, and we did not sleep together. We held hands, we kissed passionately in cars, we lay inseparably glued on moonlit beaches. We talked of marriage but we did not make love. Nice Roman Catholic young people did not have affairs. Or they didn't then, and especially not in Malta, an island steeped in the puritan ethics of the "old" church.

Since I was a small girl I had been brought up to believe that if a girl "gave in," the man eventually rejected her as chattel, even if he had said he loved her. The idea frightened my contemporaries and me so much that most of us hurtled headlong into marriage before discovering sex. A dreadful mistake.

And that spring, in that little cottage, with the morning filtering through chintz curtains and Corin's strong warm arms around me, I was still in doubt, still afraid that I might lose him if I "gave in." And I knew by now that I didn't want to lose him.

"It's all right, Dee," Corin said softly, always able to sense my moods. "It really is all right. I love you very much. You must know that. Nothing can damage those feelings. You have made me feel more in the last few weeks than I have in the whole of the rest of my life, it seems. . . ."

He looked at my mouth. Didn't kiss me. Just looked at my mouth. As though even to touch me might be too much for both of us, yet it was the thing he wanted most in the world. That was what did it. The fact that he didn't touch me, didn't rush me. Memories of the frustration of all those times in cars and on sofas with other people and the excitement and the madness of this time bubbled through my mind. I desperately wanted him to touch me. I was magnetized by his distance. I touched his mouth with my fingers, and he unpinned my hair so that it sprayed out loose across my shoulders, and he shook it so it framed my face and still he didn't touch me.

"It's up to you, Dee," he said gently. He gave me his hand and pulled me up from the sofa, took me to the door of the bedroom and showed me the elegant, chintz-covered bed, the picture window, my future.

"You can sleep here," he murmured. "I'll go back across to the other house. If that's what you want."

Then he bent his head to kiss me and it was as if the movement were in slow motion and I was watching this man whom I loved caught in some weird bend in time so that we each occupied a space apart from everything and everyone else in the world. And then I felt safe.

I think in the end it was I who closed the door behind us. I who moved toward the bed.

It was perfect. Dreamlike. More intense than I could ever have imagined. The risk, the fear of loss, the guilt evaporated. Only the moment existed. No fake morality could matter more than exploring each other, every nuance, every sensation, to yield, to be strong, to love.

Late in the morning I woke in the rumpled bed feeling dazed, exhausted but elated. Different. As though my whole body had come alive. My skin was so sensitive it could almost inhale the honeysuckle scent as it wafted in through the open window.

Hardly opening my eyes, I reached for Corin. Nothing. No wonderful warm body beside me, just tangled sheets and emptiness.

"Cor," I said sleepily. "What's happened? Where are you?"

I sat up in bed and looked around. There was no answer and no sound of activity. Suddenly I was distraught. I felt abandoned, quite alone, appalled at what I had done, ashamed of what suddenly became my weakness. Almost in tears I flung myself face down into the pillows trying to pull them over my head to shut out the light and the tumbling memories.

But when I looked up, after my first irrational panic, I saw on the pillow a single perfect rose, fresh-cut and velvet with the bloom of early summer. It was deep red, my favorite color for roses. So typical of Corin's knack for touching gestures, gifts that said more than words, which perfectly fitted the occasion, the mood, the time, the person.

"I love him," I thought to myself. "I really love him. And he loves me."

It was corny and warm and wonderful and frightening, all at the same time. I lay there basking in this wash of new sensations, suspending my mind while my feelings took over. Within a moment or two Corin appeared, tall and supple, wrapped in his father's paisley dressing gown.

"Here," he said, grinning and sitting down beside me on the bed. "Morning coffee for madame. How would she like it? Milk and two sugars? Very good then. Here you are!"

He put the coffee cups down on the bedside table, then leaned to kiss me fully on the mouth.

"Good morning, my darling," he said. "I have a surprise for you."

"Mmmmmmm," I said, curling into his arms. I am not at my best in the early morning, unlike Corin, who has always risen with the cock's crow. "Surprise? What kind of surprise?"

"My family is here," he said chirpily. "Isn't that wonderful?"

Well, he might just as well have hit me right between the eyes with a brick! I fell back onto the bed and out of his arms with a shriek of horror.

"That's too much!" I shouted. "That's just too damned much! I told you I didn't want to meet them like this! You said there'd be nobody in the cottage the whole weekend! I told you I wouldn't come if they were here. That's cheating! That's terrible!"

My bubble of happiness burst just like that. He had brought

me here under false pretenses. I had no other clothes, no tooth-brush, not even a semblance of propriety with which to mask the all too obvious situation.

"I'm furious, Corin!" I yelled. "You've misled me and betrayed me. What are you doing? What am I doing? What on earth will they think of me?"

"But it's all right, darling," said Corin soothingly, unruffled. "They'll love you. I want you to meet them. Don't get so upset. I really didn't know they'd be here, but since they are, we should make the best of it."

By this time I was sobbing and screaming in between gulps.

"You knew I wouldn't have come down to the cottage with you, wouldn't have slept with you, if I'd known we wouldn't be alone. You've tricked me and humiliated me and I feel awful—just awful!"

He tried to persuade me to come out of the studio to meet them all. But the only thing I had to wear was the creased satin suit and the high-heeled dancing shoes and black seamed stock-ings; and my makeup was smudged all over my face. I felt ridic-ulous. I knew how my own family would have felt in a similar situation—what they would have thought about a girl dressed as I was for a country weekend.

So I swung my legs out of bed and sat on the edge of the crumpled sheets, still furious at Corin.

"I'll creep off through the woods and hitch a lift back to Lon-don," I threatened. And there, hot on the heels of our first love-making, came our first almighty row. The first of many.

Suddenly Corin's face became tight and angry. He launched a counterattack.

"You've got a bourgeois mentality," he said. "You're being pathetic. My family is broadminded. They don't mind about things like that. I love you and that's the important thing. I love you and they will too."

I hoped to hell he was right. Unglueing my eyelashes with a torn Kleenex, grabbing a comb off Sir Michael's dressing table to untangle my hair, I finally summoned the courage to leave the room and try to gracefully handle what had all the hallmarks of a very ungainly introduction.

I emerged into the bright sunlight out of the dark depths of our bedroom knowing I looked like someone from a sleazy cabaret about to leap on her next client.

The sophisticated Redgraves, lucky for me, took it all in their stride. They were sweet, welcoming, loving, and appeared oblivious to the fact that I looked like a hooker. It was a wise and generous way to approach a nervous girl, and they immediately made me feel at home and a part of the family. Not a bedraggled intruder, but Corin's love. To my great relief, Sir Michael was not there, nor was Vanessa. Corin's mother, Rachel, took the first steps toward putting me at ease, and she succeeded in enchanting me straight away.

I had not anticipated her great beauty. Few photographs do her justice. Her fine-boned face with its dazzling blue eyes took my breath away. She had the firm slim body of a teenager, and her smile lit up her whole face. I forgot about my own appearance and watched her. She seemed quite unaware of her physical loveliness, and her warmth and humor dissolved all my fears. I instantly and unreservedly adored her.

She and Lynn and Corin and I sat happily under the apple tree on the lawn in the spring sunlight. Rachel, who is an inspired cook and has passed that aptitude for culinary magic on to her daughters, conjured up a delicious light lunch and Corin produced bottles of chilled white wine while Lynn and I got to know each other.

Lynn was seventeen, a pretty girl, without the striking good looks of the rest of her family, but with dancing eyes, a wicked sense of humor and an irrepressible sense of fun that drew me to her immediately. She was at drama school then, and she regaled us all with stories of her life and times there. Formality, dressing up and making up were never her style, and on this bright day she was in jeans and a shirt with her hair tied up in a pony tail, looking about twelve. When I stumblingly tried to explain my own bizarre appearance, Lynn simply laughed.

"Of course it doesn't matter," she said. "For heaven's sake, don't worry. You can borrow something of mine if you want."

But by this time I had taken off my shoes and black silk stockings and was feeling quite comfortable as I was. After lunch and a few bottles of excellent wine had been downed by the party, I felt astonishingly at home and quite spellbound by Corin's erudite family.

The Sunday newspapers were spread out over the lawn and each took turns in reading theater reviews, discussing the actors and their roles with intimate knowledge and hilarious observations. I was quite bowled over by how clever they all seemed.

Once they started talking about Vanessa's success at Stratford (where she was playing Rosalind in *As You Like It*, her first major starring role, and was attracting a great deal of media attention) and referring to famous film stars by their first names, I was addicted. A whole new world unfolded in front of my eyes.

Vanessa's acting was turning the critics upside down. She had wooed and won them without really trying, and her family was amused by the stories of how Bernard Levin, then theater critic for the Sunday *Times*, had written an article to the effect that the best thing Michael had ever done for the theater was to give birth to Vanessa!

Later I remember reading a description of Vanessa's radiant performance by writer Caryl Brahms, which also went, as Lynn said, "a bit over the top." She said that "had Shakespeare been alive to see Miss Redgrave's Rosalind, he would have written a Rosalind into every play thereafter. . . ."

Almost all the reviews of Vanessa's work were favorable. Judging by the joking naturalness with which her family treated her extraordinary success, I could not help feeling that Vanessa must be a fairly down-to-earth woman. She could hardly get away with playing the new Star in a family such as this, a home in which brains and humor seemed to come long before the trappings of fame.

When Corin and I left, late that afternoon, just as the shadows were lengthening and a breeze lifting and scattering the newspapers on the lawn, Rachel and Lynn extended warm invitations for me to visit again. And soon.

"We've loved having you," said Rachel. "And we really want you to visit us again. Corin had told us about you, and now that we know each other I want you to understand that you can come here whenever you want."

Lynn just came up and gave me a big bear hug, as though I were a sister. She made me feel very good. She is so direct. "Don't take my brother too seriously," she laughed, pulling Corin's hair. "But you can take us seriously. We really want you to come again."

I agreed to, of course, and realized with relief that I had somehow survived my appearance and made a good impression. I left feeling that what I really wanted most in the world was to become part of that family. I knew perfectly well that Corin had brought other girls down here before me, and I was determined not to be just another visitor, not just another girlfriend. I wanted to stay.

And stay I did.

But all was not a bed of roses for the loving couple. After that first crucial meeting with the family, things became complicated. Corin assumed we would continue the affair and live as lovers, either moving into my flat or his, once back in London.

I was ready for no such thing. It was still only 1962 and people had not yet begun to live together so openly as lovers. In fact it was considered quite outrageous if you had a lover, let alone lived with him.

I really didn't feel sure of Corin yet. I was afraid he wanted me only for sex. The fact that he still wanted to see me whenever he could did not assuage those doubts. There was still that inherent insecurity that I would become the discarded lover; my raging Catholic guilt gave me the terrible belief that I would be punished for the sin of loving. It wasn't a moral stand I was taking so much as a frightened gesture of self-protection. I'd given in once, but I wasn't going to be caught in that trap again, however deliciously tempting it was. And it was.

Of course, Corin's argument always was that I was being bourgeois. That I was being bound by middle-class morals, which I was. We would have endless battles of will which always finished with me pushing him away and running back to my own flat.

I really did love him, I knew that. But I wanted him to be my husband. I did not want an affair. I wanted marriage. I was so busy being afraid that all he wanted me for was my body, I had no time left to fear marriage. Marriage was just a mirage. Sex was a hard reality that I did not want to deal with until the knot was nicely tied with a platinum wedding ring.

Poor Corin. Once I had decided that all he felt for me was lust, any indication that he wanted to touch me was like a red flag to a bull. He, of course, was totally bewildered. From a sensual, inviting woman who had tumbled into bed with him in an ecstasy of erotic delight I had changed overnight into an almost frigid schoolgirl.

In my own confusion I lost sight of his. I didn't realize that he was feeling rejected and neglected or that I was behaving completely without rationale as far as he was concerned. On my part I was so afraid of losing him if I "gave in" again to my turbulent sexual feelings that I created an unnecessary and cold distance between us, which culminated in a dreadful row.

We were having dinner one evening in a small favorite bistro. After the third gulped glass of red wine I suddenly blurted out, "All you want from me is sex—I know that. Get out of my life. I never ever want to see you again!"

Corin was clutching my hand in utter astonishment, but I jerked it away, burst into tears and went running out of the restaurant.

When I got back to the flat, my roommates, both of whom had had their share of dashing suitors and dramatic exits from restaurants, tried to comfort me. The tears were still streaming down my cheeks, and I was feeling more maudlin and sorry for myself than I could ever remember.

One immediately made coffee. The other brought me cigarettes and sympathy. But all they could really do was listen. In the end it was a problem I was going to have to solve for myself, the first really significant woman's decision that I had had to make and to make alone. By the time dawn stuck its intruding light through the curtains I was utterly devastated and went to sleep feeling my instinct for self-protection must be stronger even than my love for Corin. Exhausted, convinced Corin did not want a true committed relationship (marriage), I resolved not to see him again. It was an awful thought.

But Corin must have been tossing through a similar night of angst. As I struggled into consciousness that morning it was to the shrill sound of the telephone bell.

"I've got something very important to tell you," said the familiar voice on the other end. "Will you please come and have dinner with me tonight after the show?"

"No," I said, determined not to give in and anxious to avoid further verbal abuse. Although I knew I sometimes caused scenes, I hated the emotional ordeal of having to go through them and was feeling quite drained from the night before.

"You absolutely must," said Corin. "I love you and I want to talk to you without arguments, so put on your best dress and meet me at the theater."

This time he sounded so firm, so determined, that I, half-unwillingly, half-pleased, agreed to the rendezvous. I washed my hair, went for a walk and began to feel better. By the time I'd had a bath, put on new stockings and my favorite black dress, I was ready to forget our conflict and have a wonderful evening. We did. We wined and dined and laughed.

Corin was then staying with his sister Vanessa in her antique-laden flat in Emperor's Gate, Kensington. He divided his time between there and their parents' more luxurious home in Knightsbridge, the one Corin had taken me to on the fateful night of the rhapsodic piano playing, when I had fallen headlong in love.

Tonight he took me there again. It was very quiet when we arrived, and it seemed as though there was no one at home. Giggling, we crept into the kitchen. Corin helped himself to a bottle of Sir Michael's vintage champagne from the fridge and together we went into the drawing room to drink it.

Pouring the champagne, Corin tried to articulate what he had so urgently needed to see me about.

"I've been thinking," he started. "Deirdre, I can't bear all these fights. What I'd really like is for us to . . ."

Thud. My heart almost stopped. I knew the minute he began to speak that he was asking me to marry him. That this, then, was it. This was a proposal from the man I loved. Corin too was having difficulty controlling his nervousness. He took my hand and led me out onto the balcony where a bright moon looked down on us kindly, the traffic of London flowing frantically past below us, and the champagne bubbling in our glasses.

"Well, will you marry me?" Corin demanded abruptly. And suddenly the crystal glass wobbled out of my hand, crashed onto the balcony, and spilled its contents smack on top of the unsuspecting head of a passerby. In the middle of the ensuing ruckus, with furious shouts from the people down below and both of us helpless with laughter with our arms around each other, in walked Sir Michael! He was extremely angry, as only he can be when disturbed from study or sleep.

Within seconds the romantic mood, so carefully designed, was shattered forever. Corin hadn't told his father his plans for the evening, or indeed, his life.

Michael told us briefly and sharply to be quiet, then returned to his study to resume work on the script in his hand. Corin had not known he was there; neither had thought to leave the other one of their notes that passed for communication. Had we had any idea he was at home, we would have been tiptoeing and whispering, as was the edict when Sir Michael, the master of the house, was working.

We shrugged and gave it up as a bad job. This was obviously not the moment for swearing eternal commitment. As Corin drove me home, furious with his father, he said, "Let's discuss it tomorrow. We'll go to Prunier's for lunch."

Later that night he left a note for Michael. This one read: "You have ruined my proposal and my future prospects."

But of course true love does not faint at such obstacles—it merely feints. At the elegant French restaurant of his choice the following day, over more champagne and perfect oysters, the proposal was finally accomplished.

"You know the answer," I said, with a smile that must have lit up the entire restaurant. "Of course, of course, of course, of course!"

That settled, we wandered out into the daylight, hands tightly clasped, dazed by our own bravado. We were going to get married. We were growing up. We were going to do one of those things that adults do, and make this thing we felt for each other legal. The future looked perfect.

Unfortunately for my romantic spirit, the pink-tinted haze of the day, which had so generously provided fluffy little clouds for me to walk on, was dissipated by the reality of Corin's matinee performance of *Chips with Everything*. The theater always came first.

But that night I was waiting for him when he returned from the theater. And so began a fifteen-year liaison that would only end when every avenue of hope, tolerance and love had been explored, and I finally admitted defeat in the face of my husband's commitment to politics, which, to my great distress, was more passionate than his commitment to me.

5

Living Together

Corin asked me if now I would live with him. Rather to my own surprise, I agreed. It was not a conscious gesture of defiance toward the morals of my puritan parents and upbringing; it was rather a first dipping of my toes in the heady water of independence.

Although it was thought outrageous by my parents' generation for young people to openly live together outside marriage, my own age group was just beginning to experiment with the idea of learning to know about sex, sexuality and the people you plan to swear allegiance to for the rest of your life—before you did the swearing. To me it made sense. To Corin's parents it absolutely made sense.

The Redgrave family were quite happy to accept the fact that Corin and I were living together. Far more liberal in their attitudes generally than my extremely conventional family, it seemed in no way odd to them that since we were going to get married we should live together first for a while. They considered it a completely normal and reasonable thing to do. In fact, they were quite pleased, I think, to see that their very serious son was having some fun at last. Glad, perhaps, that the loner was no longer alone.

If my own parents were slightly appalled, they were too far away to be more than shadowy ghosts of guilt on a rapidly receding horizon. As they still spent most of their time in Malta, they were unaware of the climate of social and moral change in which their children were living, and by their standards the fact that I wanted to sleep with Corin and share a home with him before the blessing of the Church had been bestowed seemed decadent. They also felt a bit in awe of the new glamorous circle I appeared to be entering. But the Redgraves handled it with such easy grace that my parents were eventually reassured that "socially acceptable" or not, in their circles, that was what was happening, and more importantly, I was very very happy.

Our decision to live together was made in an ambiance of imminent social upheaval. As Corin and I began the first serious, committed steps in our relationship, everything around us, everything we saw, listened to, touched, was changing. We were in the vanguard of a whole new movement of sexual permissiveness. If the fifties had signaled youthful rebellion, the sixties were soon to mark a revolution. Corin and I did not know it; who could have guessed how much social and political thinking would change in the last five years of the sixties? But there was an earthquake about to erupt under our feet. We lived right at the heart of the truculent flashing energy which was to transform music, fashion, art and philosophy over the next decade. We watched old ideas of morality and stability fly out the window.

The Beatles were heard in the land, and music became a riotous celebration of life and adventure. The whole tempo of the music was changing with the times, or the times with the music; it was hard to tell which came first.

Miniskirts were to symbolize the new freedom women felt and men appreciated. Short shiny haircuts highlighted the idea of nature and health as an essential path to beauty. Trouser suits for women were early indications of the strides they were taking toward their own evolution and liberation. The word "pop" was coined to apply not only to music but to lifestyles, clothes and art.

I was right there to see how art absorbed the cadence of the times and how the media turned it out again for mass consumption. I was close to a family that was part of the wave of new talent beginning to sweep through the theater and cinema. Corin's family *were* the innovators in the arts.

Vanessa had the ear and eye of the media as an actress and felt no shame in using both to proselytize her political beliefs about issues with which she was involved, such as nuclear disarmament. The man she was in love with, Tony Richardson, was turning traditional theater on its ear by never following the age-old rules of the stage.

While Corin and I wandered hand in hand down the King's Road, the Rolling Stones were being photographed by the Court photographer on the banks of the Thames. Shiny hair swung below their ears and in a short-back-and-sides world, that was thought outrageous. Youth reigned supreme, and so did young love. Drugs were not only used, they were used as a banner to proclaim the new freedom and in themselves became fashionable. "Hip" became cooler than "hep."

Politically, the young were taking a stand against the old order, beginning to insist on freedom from role playing, and taking a stand, too, on civil rights, women's rights, the rights of all minority groups—awakening, indeed, to the rights of all individuals. Freedom in the arts and freedom of the press were another battle cry. But although the atmosphere around us was becoming more relaxed and more permissive, my insecurities were still affecting the relationship between Corin and me. I wanted marriage.

So we agreed to get married as soon as the arrangements could be made. Corin did not care so much for the idea of a marriage ceremony as I did. For me a gold band on my finger was a symbol of permanence and a church wedding would satisfy my hunger for ritual acceptance into the world of grownups. All the teachings of my adolescence urged me to test this man who said he loved me by demanding a public avowal of that love. Sometimes I had nightmares that something would happen to break us up. I thought marriage would protect me. I thought if Corin swore an oath in front of a priest, then I need not be afraid of being alone again.

I knew Corin had many admirers among the pretty young actresses we met, and I seemed to hover on the edge of illogical jealousy too much of the time. Confronted by the reality of having a lover who was attractive to other women, known to other women, I felt inadequate.

I wasn't talented. I wasn't artistic. I wasn't as pretty as that one, as slim as the other, as intelligent as the third from the left. I tormented myself with the fear that I would never be able to match Corin's intellect and that there would always be someone more beautiful, more brilliant than I to catch his attention, this man so used to the attention of brilliant women.

Nothing in my education had taught me how to hold my own with either intellectuals or those who spent their lives striving to create magic from the fire of imagination. Although I could not and would not tell Corin in case he should laugh at me, I lived with the nagging fear that who I was would never be enough. It was not Corin's fault. It was my own vulnerability. Without even realizing it, I was undermining my own confidence. I could not accept the fact that he loved me as much as I loved him.

Since Vanessa's new season at Stratford, Corin had been staying more often in Vanessa's flat than in his parents' much grander London residence. Now he asked Vanessa if the two of us could live there. She had already married Tony and had moved out so she was happy for us to use it. She told Corin he could think of it as his home. We were very lucky, I realized. It was just exactly what we needed. Privacy without complications.

The bedroom had French windows which overlooked the garden. At that time of year it was wonderful to smell the fresh flowers and wander into the garden at twilight. The only problem was that I was an appalling cook. I had never been taught to cook. I enjoyed playing wife-to-be, but anything I turned my hand to was inevitably a disaster. If I didn't burn the pans, I'd burn myself on the oven and spill whatever I was holding. Corin didn't mind. He liked the Casserole restaurant by now, not the least reason being because it was our first meeting place. Dinner ended up on the kitchen floor so often that we spent most nights going out to eat.

The nicest feeling about living together was that for the first time I felt able to be completely myself within a relationship. I could just say I loved Corin and show it by making love to him. It was a great relief not to hide my feelings any more.

As I learned to adjust to day-to-day life with a man, I also gradually began to know the individual members of Corin's family.

Vanessa was becoming an extraordinary focus of attention. Among the men who fell in love with her through the power of her performances was the distinguished English theater critic Bernard Levin. He described her in *The Times* as a "goddess" and attempted to pay her court without much personal success.

Tony Richardson, the director then being hailed as the new hope of English theater and cinema, had seen Vanessa play Kate in *The Taming of the Shrew*. It was during that same season at Stratford that he, too, fell in love with the tall, tawny actress with the perfect diction and perfect blue eyes. When later he confided to me his first feeling for Vanessa, he said, "When she spoke those magnificent lines, declaring her love for Petruchio in the final scenes in a speech of unsurpassed passion and generosity, I knew that woman was for me. I had to have her."

Much to the chagrin of Mr. Levin, he did. And married her some months later.

But their marriage was under some stress even at the beginning. Both Vanessa and Tony were working very hard. Each was at that point in their careers where they had to catch the star as it came shooting their way, and ride with it. Both creatively and commercially they were stacking up their credits, but they had not completely broken through into that mysterious realm called stardom. Since each one was dedicated to a career before their meeting, it was inconceivable that anything but career should come first. But in practical terms that was difficult and frustrating. There was hardly any time to be together. Vanessa was at Stratford. Tony was in the depths of the wet West Country filming *Tom Jones.* The only time they could meet was at weekends, and often those weekends would be spent at the Redgraves' cottage in Odiham.

Their home was a flat belonging to writer John Osborne, in Shepherd's Market, right in the heart of Mayfair. But when they came to the cottage it was so obvious they were desperately in love that it was almost difficult to be with them. They are both very powerful people, and when two such people are so tuned in to each other, it can be overwhelming for everyone else. Often Corin and I would go out for walks together just to give them the space they needed. Since he and I saw each other daily, there wasn't the same urgency about the time we spent together. With Vanessa and Tony, there was such a burning intensity that you couldn't help feeling like an intruder.

Usually we would turn up at the cottage near midnight on Saturday night, as Corin was still playing in *Chips with Everything.* At Stratford the company alternates performances, and sometimes Vanessa could get away after the Friday night show, in which case she would meet up with Tony and they would drive together to the cottage. When this happened they were usually in bed by the time we arrived for our late-night cup of coffee, and they did not put in an appearance until breakfast.

Sunday breakfast was a movable feast. When every member of the family was appearing in some play or film somewhere, there were a lot of exhausted bodies on a Sunday morning. Lunch, then, was the family get-together, and Rachel would usually produce a steaming traditional English Sunday lunch, with joint of beef, roast potatoes, fresh vegetables, herbs from the garden, and a wonderful fattening pudding laden with cream.

During these lunches and family conversations, which almost

always veered in the direction of the arts or politics, Vanessa and I found we had a cause in common—the Campaign for Nuclear Disarmament. I told her I had been on marches, sit-ins, and demonstrations where she had made speeches and that I admired her courage to speak out.

My commitment to the antinuclear demonstrations of the late fifties was the first political stance I had ever taken. And it didn't feel political to me, merely common sense. My childhood had been blasted by bombs. Tales of the horrors of Hiroshima and Nagasaki had confirmed for me the abomination of conflict resolved through inflicting appalling civilian casualties. To try to stop the proliferation of nuclear weapons appeared an obvious step.

I utterly respected Vanessa's courage for publicly putting herself on the line for her beliefs. The name of Redgrave always attracted attention. At first, that was because Michael was so famous and Vanessa so beautiful. By becoming the figurehead for such a controversial movement as nuclear disarmament, she received a lot more publicity, although much of it was rather snide, and even nasty.

We would talk far into the night about our various beliefs and ideals. At this point, Corin was working behind the scenes on the political stage. He preferred, if anything, to organize, not to make speeches. Vanessa liked action, and so did I. Not long after we met, she urged me to join forces with her.

Various members of the Committee of One Hundred, who were campaigning for nuclear disarmament, discovered some secret documents showing the regional seats of government and plans for saving the lives of the Royal Family and members of Parliament in the event of a nuclear holocaust. Vanessa and I decided to have hundreds of pamphlets printed to give the public these facts, to show them that nuclear war was being considered as a serious possibility by those ruling the country, yet only that small elite group was aware of the danger and only the future survival of this group was being planned. Everyone else's survival was being ignored.

We set out to distribute the pamphlets all over London ourselves. Vanessa had the funny idea of hiding them between the
glossy pages of magazines that lay on expensive antique tables
in the lobbies of exclusive hotels like the Ritz, the Connaught
and the Savoy. It appealed to us both.

We walked into the hotels dressed in our very best and, while
idly thumbing through *Country Life, Vogue* or *The Tatler*,
slipped copies of our leaflets between the pages.

It worked extremely well. To our surprise, no one thought
we looked odd. Not once were we apprehended by angry hall
porters or doormen, and we got away with handing out handfuls
of subversive literature in the smartest hotels in London! We
piled the leftovers into telephone boxes or handed them out to
passersby in the street. It was before professional beggars and
accosters flooded the city streets, and there were no religious
pushers like the Moonies or the Hare Krishna singers. People
were only too happy to stop for a moment and chat with a
pretty woman.

Our gesture might have been juvenile, but it seemed to us to
be worth it, a beginning. We were drawing people's attention to
a hidden but existing and appalling truth. Vanessa and I were
both concerned that people be made aware that their lives were
being run by others who, in the long run, would only save themselves.

Out of this first profound anxiety about the danger of nuclear
war came Vanessa's continuing commitment to the anti-Vietnam
war movement, Black Power, the PLO and eventually the Workers Revolutionary Party. She also linked her work to her politics,
so that, for example, by backing the PLO documentary film *The
Palestinian;* by playing Fania Fenelon, the Jewish musician
forced to play while being confined in a Nazi concentration camp,
in the TV movie, "Playing for Time"; by helping the strikers in
her role as *Joan of the Stockyards*, and by infiltrating German
enemy lines during World War Two as Julia, in the movie of the
same name, she felt she was representing the persecuted.

"I choose my roles carefully," she said to me once, "so that when my career is finished, I will have covered all our recent history of oppression."

As she grew older, Vanessa, like Corin, was hardly ever light-hearted.

Lynn, on the other hand, gave her friendship with a continual touch of humor. After that first lunch at Odiham, she and I met often in London. On the nights I wasn't working we would go to the movies together while Corin was at the theater, shop to-gether and cook an occasional meal. Lynn was a far better cook than I.

Lynn had only just left her drama school, was not yet working and was still living with her parents in the family flat in Knights-bridge. After Michael finished his performance in *Out of Bounds*, he would sometimes take us out for dinner. But one afternoon, on his way home from a matinee performance in the West End, he was blocked by an enormous commotion in the Mall. He had been caught up in the midst of howling mobs pursuing the fleeing Queen Frederika of Greece, yelling epithets like "Nazi scum" and "Go home, traitor." Michael, the perfect gentleman, was horrified to see a woman treated in this way, and arrived home trembling with shock and anger.

Corin, naturally, endorsed the crowd's action. He felt that people were rightly expressing their rage against a known fas-cist. Lynn and I were on Corin's side, which increased Michael's anger to such a pitch that he suddenly rose from his chair and, in thundering Shakespearean tones, announced to Corin that he no longer considered him his son, that he should leave his home forever. Michael's power of delivery is rightfully famous! It was a frightening sight to behold. At this juncture, a tearful Lynn leaped to her feet announcing that if Corin was no longer his son, then she no longer was his daughter. The three of us, somewhat taken aback by the turn of events, then trooped rather uncer-tainly out of the room, into Lynn's car and back to our own home.

We sat drinking coffee, Corin and I trying to pacify Lynn, who was extremely upset, and explored the alternatives of what to do next. We wondered how serious Michael was and, on remembering the expression on his face, decided that he was extremely serious. The only thing to be done was for Lynn to stay with us until she could find a flat of her own. We started to worry about how Rachel would feel. Perhaps we had been hasty in stomping out in the way that we had.

As we were preparing to settle down for the night, the phone rang. It was Michael. He was as upset as we were over the row. He apologized and invited us all out to dinner the following evening as a reconciliation. In family upsets, if he felt he had been unfair or unkind, he never found it difficult to apologize—something I found rare in people of his generation.

Lynn returned home much comforted, and the following evening Corin, Lynn, Michael and I had a gourmet celebration.

Sir Michael was not always easy to get along with. His moods, sometimes dark, would alienate him from the people around him. Often he would become impenetrable and aloof even with his own children, who still lived to some extent in awe of him. As time went by these moods became more frequent and the man more alienated. But in the early stages of my relationship with the family, he was still able and willing to come out of his shell to be charming. Family social occasions were his favorite times.

At the inevitable formal lunch when both families were introduced to one another before Corin and I were married, it was Michael whose flair as a host saved the day from embarrassment or awkward silences. It was also the first time that I made a really strong personal contact with my future father-in-law.

The lunch was held at Michael and Rachel's flat. With some trepidation, my parents and I arrived at the appointed time.

It was a bit nerve-racking. Our two families had very different frames of reference. The only thing bringing all these people together under one roof was the fact that two of their respective children were in love with each other and wanted to get married. The fact that we were the catalysts of this event caused a certain amount of predictable tension in both Corin and me. We felt shy, nervous and anxious about the outcome.

But Michael was undaunted. When he is in form he can be the

wittiest, most generous man one can ever hope to meet. Because of his own hypersensitivity, he has the ability to relate well to other people's feelings of shyness and inadequacy. He helped my parents to relax by opening bottle after bottle of champagne and toasting Corin and me at every opportunity. Throughout the lunch, he seemed to sense every time I had a moment of panic, and he gave me warm smiles of reassurance. When finally the time came to depart, Michael put his arm around my shoulders as we walked to the door. "I am very pleased about the engagement," he said, smiling down at me. "You are both very young, I know, but you are so happy, it's wonderful to see." I hugged him and remembered the first time I had met him in their Knightsbridge flat, and my lasting impression.

Terribly nervous and breathlessly impressed by meeting such a luminary of the stage, I should think I was probably rather sycophantic. But if I was, he never made me feel silly. And if I was, it was because he truly impressed me as a great man.

His presence is that of a gentleman. He has that peculiar gift, which few people possess, which is to make the person to whom he directs his attention feel like the lucky recipient of special treasures. He embodies an astoundingly magnetic quality, charisma, an almost lethal charm.

Of all the men I knew, only Corin was able to convey that same sense of occasion, of magic, in a first meeting. Perhaps it is one of the guarded secrets of great actors, and perhaps to them a hundred people are the same as one. Loved, loving, but in the end just part of the audience.

✿ 6 ✿

Wedding

There didn't seem to be a reason for crying. I just couldn't stop the tears. On the eve of my wedding day, I felt I was standing at a crossroads still trying to read the signpost to the road I had already chosen. I kept remembering what a girlfriend had once told me about marriage, how you really believe the vows you're making at the time you're making them. How you stand in the church, nicely programmed by society, assessing your bond as unique and beautiful. You publicly promise you will never sleep with anyone else but this man until the day you die. At the time it feels right because it's the public gesture you want to make to show your love.

You start as a willing slave, still believing the dream, wanting to worship, wanting approval, clamped into society's idea of "love." You learn to cook, iron his shirts, have his babies, build up his confidence, create a secure background for your family and his career. He begins to advance in the world just as you are being reduced to cook, nappy changer and chief drudge. My friend's choice of what happened next was limited—join the army of wives on tranquilizers and pretend it's all okay.

I groaned inwardly. I wanted it all to be different. But in that last-minute panic, marriage, which had always seemed to be a lifejacket, suddenly also became a kind of death—the end of being young, irresponsible, carefree. Although the indulgence of those luxuries had run its course and been found insubstantial and insufficient for real happiness, I was suddenly apprehensive about my ability to perform in a more mature role.

Along with the proverbial bridal jitters, I was all too aware of an added dimension in my personal situation. I was about to marry into a famous acting family—not so simple as getting married to the boy next door. The whole matter of fame seemed suddenly to color everything, success setting the Redgraves apart from all my known realities. "How well equipped am I to deal with that?" I wondered. "Am I going to be able to hold my own with Vanessa? She is so strong." Corin's view of ideal womanhood was personified in Vanessa, and I knew that was going to be a hard one to live up to.

Traditionally it has always been the province of the male to indulge in a last night of freedom panic. But in our case it was Corin comforting me, rather than having a wild night on the town with his men friends.

I was staying with my parents at the home of family friends. Corin called me from the theater just before he was going on. Although my mother answered the telephone to try to block his hearing my desolate voice, he insisted on talking to me, reassuring my fears with his confidence.

I sat in the hall crouched over the telephone and trying desperately to pull myself together enough to even talk to him. I sputtered my confusions into the receiver. "It's not that I don't want to get married, it's that I'm finding it hard to get in perspective the reality that by tomorrow I'm going to *be* married, I'm going to be Mrs. *Redgrave* . . ."

"You silly idiot," he said. "I don't care whether we get married or not. You're already part of the family. You're the one who couldn't cope with just living together. I want to live with you so I agreed to get married but I don't think it will change the way we feel about each other at all."

It was exactly what I needed to hear. A sharp slice of earthy common sense to pull me out of the miasma of emotion that threatened to drown not just me, but my whole family!

I managed to make it to bed without further histrionics. My mother tucked me in as though I were fifteen years old again, and it felt comforting.

"Whoever said that marriages were made in heaven must have been an atheist," she said, smiling at me. "Just don't expect too much from yourself or Corin. On the evidence to hand I'd say you've chosen well. He seems to be an intelligent man who knows exactly when to offer the flowers or wield the whip with you. I just hope he knows what he's let himself in for!"

I hugged her and we both laughed.

But when she switched the light out I didn't sleep. I was exhausted, but every time I shut my eyes images would race across the lids, jerking me back into consciousness.

It didn't seem as though I had slept at all when light was coming through the windows and my mother came breezing through the door looking braced for the occasion and determined to cheer me.

"Coffee, darling," she said firmly, and set a mug of steaming brew beside me.

A ray of white August sunlight slanted like a laser beam through the room and picked out the white organza ruffles of my wedding dress. The dress was short, with a stiffened skirt down which the light slid, and it had a matching coat. I had thought the outfit perfectly proper and rather glamorous when my mother and I bought it. Now the dress and coat looked like those paper-cutout clothes for dolls.

As I sat in front of the dressing table, I could hear the sounds of a household in uproar through the crack of the open door. My mother had placed heady bowls of brilliant summer flowers on every available space. There was a scent of roses and lilies mixed with my mother's perfume, hanging like incense in the air. All the surfaces of the antique tables were polished like shining copper, and this smell lingered too.

It reminded me that I was the one who was still not polished and perfumed, ready for my final exit as a single woman.

I jammed a cigarette in my mouth and wished my father would turn up with the glass of brandy I so badly needed. Looking in the mirror I wondered who on earth that was, staring back at me.

Just as I was fixing my hat (actually it wasn't a hat, it was a single enormous white silk rose which I pinned to the front of my beehive hairdo) my father came into the room.

"Looks like a miner's lamp doesn't it, Dad?" I grinned at him through the looking glass.

He meanwhile had tripped over my half-filled suitcase, and was hopping around on one foot clasping his ankle in mock agony.

"Well, thank God I've only got one daughter," he said. "I never want to go through this madness again in my entire life!"

And taking an affectionate swipe at my behind, he opened the door and yelled out to my mother, "Where's my bloody tie, Diana? If I've got to give away my daughter the least you can do is see that I'm properly dressed!"

Then he winked at me and closed the door, moving across the room to where I sat, pulling up a chair and taking a deep swig of the glass of champagne he had just brought for me.

"So I've got you off my hands at last, have I?" he asked, twinkling at me. "Never thought I'd do it, I'll tell you that."

I could see Dad was beginning to enjoy acting out his father of the bride role. I got up from the dressing table, and trying hard not to shift my coiffure or rumple my dress, put my arms around him for a hug.

It was always very difficult for my father to show affection. I knew in my heart of hearts that he was proud of me, but it was so hard for him to articulate his feelings. More often than not it was up to me to cross the distance his shyness created between us.

"I love you, Dad," I whispered.

"Me too," he said gruffly, then thrust the glass into my hand. "Here, take a sip of this. Steady your nerves, my girl."

He waited with me, not talking much, just being there, while I put the finishing touches to my makeup. When finally I was ready, he took my arm firmly in his. To my surprise he really looked at me, held me away from him for a moment, then said carefully, "I think you look perfectly beautiful, Deirdre." He turned me around so I could see myself in the mirror again. "You are a woman now. Of course. I've been thinking about you as a little girl far too long."

And that was as far as he would go. But I knew that it meant he loved me, and it was enough.

The exquisite portico of the church was bathed in sunlight. But the long walk up the aisle was jammed with photographers and television cameras. I hadn't expected quite so many. I was suddenly being treated as a celebrity and it frightened me. I felt fake. It wasn't my fame they were after, it was the Redgraves'. I had done nothing to arouse all this interest except to marry one of them.

I clung to my father's arm and we bludgeoned our startled way through the exploding flashbulbs while I looked around wildly for some sign of Corin. Of course we were late, and he was already at his place in the church, waiting.

Corin and I had had several rows over the wedding ceremony. Still very religious at that time, I desperately wanted to be married in a church; Corin could hardly be convinced to even set foot inside one. We finally compromised on the Actors' Church. I was happy and Corin more comfortable with the idea of a church wedding.

Once inside the musty darkness, I saw at the end of the aisle the outline of Corin's head silhouetted against the light from the altar candles. I hoped he would be as moved as I by the cere-mony.

He turned and grinned at me reassuringly. I needed it. My fears began to subside a little. The hymn we had chosen, "Jeru-salem," started softly on the organ.

As I walked up the aisle I saw Michael out of the corner of my eye. Although he wasn't wearing a morning coat (we had decided to dispense with that formality at least) he still managed to look extraordinarily distinguished. And big. The bearing of both him and Corin makes them stand out. Perhaps it is simply the still-ness of their elegance.

Behind me I could hear the sound of muffled sobbing. Who was that? Not my mother, surely; she always controls her emotions. No, it was my two best friends, Sue and Trisha Locke, my com-panions since childhood days in the hot sun of Malta. We had shared a flat, boyfriends, clothes and secrets. They were crying for me, for us, for lost youth and the beginning of womanhood.

Even Corin had tears in his eyes. I knew the ritual had touched a chord in him and I wanted to reach out, to stroke his hair, to tell him that everything was fine. But I had the feeling that it was all happening to someone else, as if I were hovering above the scene and recording my life for someone else's poster-ity.

When the vicar asked Corin if he would take me for his lawful wedded wife, the old man forgot my name and called me Desiree. Suddenly Cor's resonant voice rang out through the church, say-ing, "No. I'll take Deirdre as my lawful wedded wife."

"Personally," I whispered to Corin, "I rather like the name Desiree."

Almost the entire remainder of the service passed in a blur. I must have answered correctly and made the right moves because within moments, it seemed, I was following Corin in to sign the register and I could see a gold ring burning new and strangely bright on the fourth finger of my left hand.

As the vicar pushed the register in front of me to sign in my new name, I kept thinking over and over again, "I have a husband. I have a new name. Why is it only women who give up their own names?"

But nudged by Corin, I snapped out of it again, leaving the thought to be digested with the rest of the day's events. Later, much later.

The wedding march boomed through the church as we matched our steps to its thunderous rhythm. I was Mrs. Redgrave.

Outside the church, I could see a phalanx of photographers and unknown faces pressing against the railings that looped the church. In the bright sunlight, the families assembled in all their wedding finery. The Redgraves and the Hamilton-Hills grouped themselves carefully in front of the camera and waited for me to take my place beside Corin in the center.

I went into a sort of automatic gear. The cameras, of course, were trained on the Redgraves. The moment Vanessa appeared, I could hear the whirring as she turned and the flashbulbs blinded me for minutes on end.

Vanessa was on a rare break from her season at Stratford. She was used to handling this kind of situation and did it with grace and an actress' eye for the spotlight.

I, on the other hand, was totally unprepared. It was the first time I had had to deal directly with the kind of attention that fame and public scrutiny could bring. I felt as though I were stepping onto the set of the Redgraves' movie—as an extra.

All three of the Redgrave women were wearing bright summer dresses and straw hats. But it was Vanessa who stole the show. She dominates situations, exuding a charismatic power with which she controls people's attention. Like a blond Amazon, she towered above us. Six feet tall and as blue-eyed as her father, she has an almost masculine presence, as though in another life she would have been wielding a sword.

"Now we're sisters, Dee," she told me warmly. "Stop looking so petrified." She reached to adjust the rose in my hair, waving away photographers as she did. "This is *your* day. Enjoy it. I'm sure you'll be wonderfully happy with Corin, and I wish you both all my love and the best of happiness."

Lynn came running up to embrace me. "Congratulations, both of you. It's wonderful. You both look wonderful. I love you both!"

Corin stood beside me with a grin on his face that stretched from ear to ear, like a child who has just been given an ice cream. To me he looked about twelve years old.

In fact he hardly spoke one word between the church and the car, and it wasn't until we had both been pushed and shoved into its dark interior that he suddenly put his arm around my shoulders and kissed me properly for the first time that day.

"I love you, Mrs. Redgrave," he said. "How do you feel now?"

"Sick as a parrot," I replied. "Where's the champagne? This is all getting a bit much for me. How are you?"

"Actually I could use a glass, too." His face was tense. The smile was still there but he looked like I felt—in need of some alcoholic beverage to steady the nerves.

The limousine swept through the sun-drenched streets. People peered in at us as the car stopped at traffic lights or became trapped between juggernauts as we tried to get to our champagne. Smiling, curious faces, hands waved in greeting or blessing, a scowl or two, and one old woman who touched the crossed white ribbons in the front for luck. There were so many people and smiles and cameras and well-wishers and cameras and smiles floating past. It all became dreamlike again, as though we were moving underwater. Corin felt it too and kept his arm firmly around me.

Once we got to the reception, it became more like being on stage than ever. My parents had insisted on the traditional rituals, so Corin and I had to line up for the handshakes and wet cheek kisses. There were so many hands, so many "Hellos" and "How are you's," and by the end of it Corin and I were limp.

At this point the family Redgrave came into its own. Michael gave us his personal wedding presents. Corin's was a beautiful cameo ring set in gold. Mine, a necklace of seed pearls and coral.

Both were exquisitely made, chosen with Michael's perfect taste. I was completely taken aback. I don't know what I had expected, but not such care, such extraordinary thoughtfulness. It was a very emotional moment for all three of us. We just put our arms around each other and hugged without words. Then Michael drew back and, slightly tearfully, kissed me on each cheek.

Until now I had always had the impression that because Michael so dominated the family, was such a patriarch, he had somehow cut off his children from direct or emotional communication. His authority, and their respect for it, isolated him too much from his offspring. But at this moment, he suddenly seemed as approachable as any father.

Across the room I could see Vanessa talking to my parents. I noticed that throughout the afternoon she made a point of spending time with all of my family, and I was glad. She and Corin had always been so close throughout childhood and adolescence, although her recent marriage to Tony interfered with the amount of time they now spent together. I knew that, aside from me, Vee (as I also came to call her) was absolutely the closest person to Corin. I wasn't sure how she would take this new commitment on his part.

It reassured me to see her, blue eyes blazing, chatting animatedly with my mother, swapping stories with my younger brothers and toasting my father. For the first time I believed she was genuinely delighted at the match, that her brother's love for me touched her. She is not, I was to discover, a woman who betrays her innermost feelings easily. She is extraordinarily guarded, like Corin.

Sometimes her looks border on those of a buxom, ruddy-faced farm girl; sometimes she appears quite plain; but today she was at her best, when her bone structure and mobility of expression took over to create a strong distinctive beauty.

Even the humorlessness which sometimes pervades her entire being had taken flight for the day. It is as easy for her to veer from extremes of chill disapproval to extremes of warmth and charm, as it is for her father, physically so like her, to alter from inhibited isolation to sparkling conviviality.

I sensed then that Vanessa wanted to know me better and that we would become very close friends, but it would always be difficult for me to pierce the inner shell. It is easy, I realize now, to know the superficial Vanessa, and very, very difficult to know the creature beneath the glowing surface.

I wandered over to where Lynn was sitting on the windowsill, sipping champagne and looking out over the garden as the sun began to pale and the shadows to flick over the perfectly manicured lawns.

"Hey," she said as I came up to her, "how are you doing, Dee? Ready for wifedom yet?"

"You," I said, putting my arms around her, "are now the only unmarried Redgrave. Anyone here you like the look of? Anyone you'd especially like me to introduce you to, since this is a day of new beginnings?"

She looked around at the motley crew of relations, friends, actors and stockbrokers. Flushed perspiring faces and a roar like the Tower of Babel hardly shed a romantic light on any of the possibilities. Just as we were about to do our usual quick rundown on the available talent, there was a fierce hammering as her father rapped on the table and called for silence.

"Time for telegrams, speeches, and—wait for it—cutting the cake," said Michael to the assembly.

"He's risen to the occasion," I whispered to Lynn, giggling.

"He always does," she said. "He might not be a great conversationalist when he's at home, but put him on stage or in a spotlight and there's no holding him back."

So I sat with Lynn as the telegrams were read out. Michael, my father and Corin all made speeches, my father feeling somewhat overawed by the illustrious company although he was used to speechmaking and normally rather enjoyed it.

Rachel was standing near Lynn and me, and as my father began to talk, leaned over and said, "What an extraordinarily handsome man your father is, Deirdre. I felt very proud walking back down the aisle on his arm. He is quite one of the most charming escorts I've had in a long time, my dear."

Corin and I cut the cake, passed slices around the room, left ours untouched, and chattered brightly with whoever caught our attention first. The champagne flowed, the day grew fuzzier.

To my surprise and delight my dear husband had planned a romantic honeymoon for the one full night available to us as Corin's break from *Chips*.

He knew I wanted this night to be special, even if there were only a few hours of it, so he had booked us a room in a Paris hotel and drove me to the airport in a state of delighted anticipation.

What he had completely forgotten was that I cannot bear flying. I am a craven coward when it comes to going anywhere near those great steel birds in the sky. It was our first moment of crunch as a married couple. What do I do? Let him down forever by my cowardice? Or allow him to continue to think of me as an adventuress, a great experimenter with life?

We split the difference. I curbed my panic, downed three stiff brandies, and he practically carried me to the plane.

I survived to see Paris and to experience it for one night as a honeymoon lover. We followed the storybook guide. We made love in our ancient French double bed, we drank wine by the Seine, wandered through the cobbled streets of the Left Bank on a cloud of euphoria, squabbled over dinner.

At breakfast time the next morning we kissed in between the bites of croissant and read how the English Sunday papers had made our wedding out to be Vanessa's great day.

"Vanessa Steals the Day" blared the headlines. The national press published pictures of both the bride and Vanessa. It was my first taste of fame and reflected glory. I wasn't quite sure then whether Vanessa was reflecting my glory or I was simply being allowed to bask in hers.

Either way I did not like it much.

"Trust your sister to be the star of my wedding day!" I said to Corin, slightly cross.

"Don't be silly, darling," said my husband, completely unaware of the prick to my ego. "You'd better learn to pay absolutely no attention to the press. If you do take what they print seriously you'll become a neurotic wreck."

He leaped out of bed, pulling me with him, giving me little time to reflect on the wisdom of his words. The time to reflect would come later, as I struggled to maintain my own identity in a family of stars. Now I was content to let my husband shower me with love and attention, so the newspaper articles receded into the background of my mind.

Corin even had time to buy me some lingerie in the Faubourg St.-Honoré. We raced in a cab toward the airport. And by the time we landed back in London I thought I was more or less ready for wifedom.

We would continue to live in the flat Vanessa had given us. It suited us perfectly with its huge drawing room and wonderful big bedroom overlooking a dense private garden. It was not, however, so big that I couldn't handle it as a housewife.

We drove from the airport to Sloane Square. Corin's date with Mr. Chips came first. Feeling lonely, I climbed out of the cab when it reached our home, my mind preoccupied with menus and how they could be transferred from French parchment and scrolled writing into something that would be waiting for Corin when he got home from the theater. I had great ideas of becoming the Perfect Wife.

So absorbed was I in this myth, however, that I failed to go to the one room I should have. Instead I wandered forlornly into the bedroom, beginning halfheartedly to unpack.

I could almost smell those snails in garlic, and the thought drew me to the kitchen, where I found that my darling Corin had stocked the larder with food and the empty fridge with champagne. He had filled the living room with flowers.

His thoughtfulness took me completely by surprise. I hadn't expected him to anticipate my own anticlimax. Feeling loved and wanted and capable of responding again, I opened one of the bottles beaded with frost. Then I drew myself a bounteous bubble bath and prepared for my husband's return in a froth of scented water and a cloud of happiness, vintage champagne in hand.

7

Learning to Be a Redgrave

The rest of my introduction to life as a Redgrave was not luxurious. Corin's lowly position as a pupil in stagecraft at the Royal Court meant that his earnings were minimal. Although *Chips with Everything* was an enormous critical success, the Royal Court Theater, however prestigious in the art world, was not the West End. Actors played there for very little money and felt lucky to do so. Corin was always more concerned with the integrity of his work than its financial rewards, and I respected him for that, even if it did put a constant strain on our purse strings. When he had lived at his parents' flat in Knightsbridge, he had few expenses, so could afford nights out at a café or a restaurant. He did not get an allowance from his parents. Running our first home together required most of Corin's weekly paycheck. After two or three weeks of married life, I had to get a job too.

As before, our hours were tailored to his performances, and our lives lived upside down in relation to the schedules of most people with normal nine-to-five jobs. When other people were getting up, we were usually going to bed. Our romantic moments were not spent in candlelit restaurants but at raucous lunches in workmen's cafés, where we'd eat heartily of sausages and chips and hold hands under the plastic tabletops.

By the cocktail hour, when most good Kensington housewives were producing their first chilled martini of the evening for the work-weary husband, Corin was slipping into his *Chips with Everything* persona and I was scrubbing the kitchen floor preparatory to setting out for my own part-time occupation.

To supplement our rather boring diet of bread and cheese alternating with boiled eggs (I still couldn't get them right— they were either swimming in jellied mucus, or hard as acorns), I took part-time work as a waitress in a rather smart little café called The Stock Pot, in Piccadilly.

It did not worry me that I had to work. I took it as a matter of course that to nudge Corin's budding career on its way, I would do my part to help support us. I wanted a job with hours that would dovetail with my husband's time spent at the theater, so that rather than sitting at home alone in the evenings I could occupy my time and earn some money as well. Corin, for his part, would have my company during the day, when he was not working.

There was no stigma attached to waitressing in that day. Many a discreet bustling little restaurant in Knightsbridge boasted waitresses with the same accents as the shoppers from Harrods. In Chelsea, titled heads would jostle one another for tips. In Mayfair the Hermès scarves tangled with the Jacqmar silks as young ladies of breeding earned themselves pocket money and their establishments earned the reputation of being somewhat like a club, only less expensive.

The organization I worked for had a small chain of coffee bars and restaurants staffed by demure debutantes, fiancées-in-waiting for Guards Officers to return from postings abroad, and rather classy actresses, like Georgina Hale, about to be discovered by the Royal Shakespeare Company. One of the girls I worked with was Grace Coddington, who won the *Vogue* new model competition while she was there and years later went on to become the magazine's fashion editor.

Nobody, least of all the Redgraves, who were hardly offering us an alternative in the shape of house or allowance, objected to my occupation.

During the day The Stock Pot catered to secretaries in patent-leather pumps with gilt chains across the instep or heel, and to earnest young men in pin-striped suits, usually apprenticed to stockbrokers or law firms in St. James's. It was clear they would soon be able to afford business lunches down the road at Wheeler's, but for the moment they had no expense accounts and had to slide by on a quick bowl of soup and espresso coffee with two spoonfuls of Demerara sugar.

After dark was rather a different scene, and it certainly opened my eyes. The Stock Pot during evening hours became a center for Piccadilly's bizarre night life. Performers from the nearby clubs and cabarets came to eat and gossip, and to my surprise I found the nucleus of this after-dark world was homosexual. The gay scene in London was still firmly under wraps in 1963. To come across it unwrapped was quite fascinating.

Corin, however, was extremely discomfited by the "girls." He would come to collect me after the theater, neat and handsome in his Wesker haircut, reading the paper with his glasses perched on the end of his nose, looking a bit like a professor of English at a boy's prep school. He was so good-looking that the queens loved him. They would save him a place at their table, and then proceed to tease him unmercifully. Even with all his sophistication he never quite got used to it.

The tips, I must say, were not particularly generous, so I did not contribute enormously to the comfort of our domestic life or the size of our personal budget. In fact, we both became remarkably thin, and sheer hunger drove us to extremes we sometimes regretted.

One day I opened our door to find a parcel sitting on the steps. It was elegantly wrapped, and addressed to me. Startled, I took it inside and began to undo it, thinking it must be a late wedding present. When I had unraveled all the paper I came to a heavy china pot. Written across the top in a flourishing antique script were the words Fortnum & Mason's Finest Beluga Caviar. I could not believe my eyes. We had not eaten properly for days. Clutching the pot as though I'd never let it go, I bounded into our tiny kitchen and plunked the caviar down on the drainboard in front of my husband and teenage brother Rob, who was visiting.

"Food!" I cried. "At last we can eat!"

"What is it?" asked Corin cautiously, looking at the pot as though it were a bomb.

"Caviar," announced my brother triumphantly. "This is Beluga caviar."

It took us about two seconds to register our good fortune. With rumbling stomachs we rushed to the supermarket.

"Eggs," I said, "for hard-boiling. I can try hard-boiled eggs again. I'll chop them up really fine, and we need some sour cream."

"And lemons," said Corin firmly.

Grasping the goodies purchased with our last pennies, we scrambled home again, mouths watering. We shot through the door, slammed on the water for the eggs, sliced lemons so fast I barely noticed my cut finger, and had eaten the entire fifty pounds' worth of prime Russian caviar fifteen minutes later.

Just as we each drew breath, rubbing our stomachs and pushing the remains of the thin toast aside, the telephone rang. It was Diana Hanbury, my parents' old friend.

"Hello Diana," I said, surprised. We did not hear from her very often and I hadn't seen her since the wedding.

"Deirdre, my dear," she said. "I'm just ringing to check that you received a parcel today."

"What parcel would that be, Diana?" I inquired politely but with heart sinking to my bursting stomach.

"It's some caviar for Rob to take back to Malta as a present to the surgeon who just performed an operation on me," she explained. "I'm just confirming that you've got it, and Rob will take it out to Malta with him when he flies off to the island tomorrow."

There was stunned silence.

"C-caviar," I stuttered. "Oh . . . caviar . . . yes. Well, I hate to have to tell you, Diana, but we've eaten it."

"You've what?" she said appalled. "Deirdre, are you being serious?"

There was another embarrassed silence.

"I'm afraid so, Diana. There was no letter with it, it just seemed like a gift from heaven."

"But it's teatime, you can't eat caviar at teatime!" she said hopefully.

"Well, we have, Di, it seemed such a wonderful change from cheese," I mumbled.

I was embarrassed at our mistake, but secretly delighted that we had finished it all before we knew the truth. Diana rose to the occasion with typically British aplomb. "If things have been so bad," she said, "I am taking you and Corin out to the Caprice for lunch tomorrow and you can have as much caviar as you like!"

Since Corin and I were both too proud to ask our parents for money and took great pride in our financial independence most of the time, it was really only at weekends that we ate well. Then Rachel would invite us to Odiham, where she feasted her family lavishly, or we went to Sunday lunch with Tony and Vanessa in their enormous white Regency house in fashionable St. Peter's Square, Chiswick.

Corin and I were, in fact, frequent guests at the Richardsons' London house during this first year of our marriage. I found it exhilarating. Tony and Vanessa, a beautiful couple among stars, seemed to epitomize the world's idea of the "Beautiful People." The fact that I was now part of this set surprised me a little. But I was beginning to learn the real power of the Redgrave name, magic to conjure with.

A Redgrave was welcome at any social gathering. I was astonished at how many people paid homage to fame, but somehow I could never feel quite comfortable with it. It was fun to be part of an elite circle, but I always had that slight feeling of inferiority which comes with marrying a "name" or title, rather than being

84

born to it. Try as I would to maintain a sophisticated front, too often I felt like the barely tolerated country cousin. To Corin, however, Vanessa was merely his beloved sister and also a damned good cook, a skill she had learned from Rachel. Since most of our domestic meals consisted of baked beans on toast (I could open tins), or bowls of vegetable soup at The Stock Pot, Corin's desire to attend Vanessa's luncheons and soirees was understandable. He was oblivious to the glitter of the company, absorbed by the succulence of the food!

Most of all I enjoyed the company of Tony. He had the knack of being able to turn even the most commonplace situation into an event. Tall and wiry, always dressed in an American bomber jacket and white Levi's, he was not particularly good-looking, but his energy and magnetism could transform everyone and everything around him. Socializing was a perfect way for him to relax. He was fascinated by people, so when he stopped directing them on stage or on screen, he would draw them into his house to play and, I always thought, to observe the interaction.

The entertainments were lavish. The best champagne stocked the fridge, there were flowers everywhere, and the food met his most exacting culinary demands. People flocked to the Richard-sons' dinner table.

But Tony's wit, sharp as it was, was often at other people's expense, and I felt glad that he and I had formed an immediate and close friendship. I would have felt unequal to dealing with the cutting edge of his humor had it been directed against me.

I quickly became closer to Tony than to the rest of my in-laws. My immediate and strong rapport with him was to help me deal with the newness of those early days as a Redgrave, months when he too was being freshly initiated into the family circle. Like me, he was a Redgrave in one way; in another, he was not. We shared that state of confused identity, although for him, hanging onto his own identity was far simpler as he was an established artist in his own right.

Tony could easily have afforded a cook in those days. But like

Rachel, Vanessa really enjoyed cooking, felt it to be part of her womanly attributes that should be used, shared, given to those she loved. So she insisted on keeping servants at bay, although I know it worried Tony that she would arrive from Stratford exhausted in the early hours of Sunday morning, sleep briefly, produce enormous meals for family and friends, playing gracious hostess until she returned to Stratford once more for the next performance.

But Vanessa's energy was boundless, and in those days she loved her role as Tony's wife. With her work allowing so little time to be with him, she did not want servants intruding on their privacy, and in all the time I've known her she has never had cooks, housekeepers or chauffeurs, as her parents had, although later, when she had children, she did have a nanny for them while she was away working.

The Richardson house was enchanting. The plain whitewashed walls were covered with valuable paintings. Next to them political posters hung incongruously—of Castro and the Campaign for Nuclear Disarmament.

Large white comfortable sofas sat on Wilton carpets. Shelves full of interesting books lined the walls. Plants trailed and spilled and blossomed everywhere. Bowls full of flowers brightened every corner, as did Tony's eccentric collection of rare birds; a toucan and several mynah birds jabbered constantly whenever you walked by.

By then Tony had formed Woodfall Films with John Osborne. The two were considered the Great White Hopes of British films and in the vanguard of what was becoming known as the New Wave in British cinema. The actors, writers and directors who came to the house, from John Osborne, Karel Reisl and producer Oscar Lowenstein to David Hemmings, Rita Tushingham and John Dexter, now production adviser at New York's Metropolitan Opera, were all part of that new wave in the arts. I sat silently, fascinated, listening to their discussions on style, mood, technique, writing, learning as much as I could about the cultural explosion taking place in our city, glad to be at the heart of it.

Tony and Vanessa went to Cuba. They returned full of enthusiasm for the new regime, bringing back with them one of South America's leading film directors, Alberto Roldan. As Vee was busy and Tony frequently away, she asked us if we would help take care of her guest and he soon moved in with Corin and me. Alberto was an interesting man. He had supported Castro in his fight to overthrow Batista, and was full of stories of the revolution.

As he talked to us so passionately, he painted a thrilling picture of a potential utopia. He believed that the Cuban spirit had managed to evade the potential excesses of revolution, bureaucracy, puritanism, and that somehow the revolution worked because everyone felt it was for a common cause—that all would benefit, one way or another.

Over the years, he would become disenchanted. As always, reality proved tougher than the dream.

It was typical of Vee that she would find a revolutionary, fall in love with both hero and cause, drag the revolutionary home with her to start the business of changing the world together with him, then find she had other things to do. It was in this whirlwind of carelessness that Corin and I found ourselves with more than one of Vee's protégés. She moved so quickly from one cause, one passion, to another, that it was hard for people to understand that her commitments seemed to last only as long as the drama of that moment.

I grew to resent what Tony euphemistically described as Vanessa's absent-mindedness. I felt her casual attitude toward other human beings bordered on selfish indifference. But because I was so shy and so in awe of Corin's family, it took me a while before I plucked up the courage to openly challenge Vanessa the humanitarian.

It was quite difficult, I think, for Corin to understand my attitude. Once or twice I tried to explain that I thought the Redgraves lived in the sort of golden bubble inhabited by the famous and successful.

Scott Fitzgerald wrote about the division between the very

rich and the not so rich, I would remind Corin. Fame is much the same. It sets people apart by imbuing them with a sense of superiority. That very inaccessibility attracts others.

Power of any kind is an erotic magnet to some people, and its force should not be underestimated.

What was harder to explain was my own nagging sense of futility, thrown as I was into this peculiarly unreal world, this galaxy in which I felt I had no function. On the one hand, I felt I was intruding on their privileged lifestyle; on the other hand I was impressed enough to want to share it. But there were years to go before I felt more interesting than a lucky outsider singled out for a personal glimpse into their enchanted world.

Corin wanted, expected, me to adore his beautiful family as much as he did. He could not understand my misgivings. While I sat at dinner at the Richardson home, agonizing inside over what I was beginning to see as an erosion of my own identity, Corin would nibble on a piece of chicken Kiev, perfectly rolled by Vanessa, swirl white wine in a fine-stemmed glass and address his almost perfect mind to the intellectual preoccupation of the moment.

"I'm a lesser mortal," I confided to Corin sorrowfully, when we were lying in bed talking after one of the Richardson soirees. "Your entire family shines with success. What am I to do? I am a waitress in a Piccadilly café and I definitely do not shine."

Corin just smiled, rolled over, hugged me, rumpled my hair, would not take it seriously. "Everyone is a star," he'd say lightly. "You're a star, my darling. I'm a star. One day you'll glitter with *my* success and then I'll buy you caviar for breakfast and venison for tea. Will that make you happy? Will you wait for our very own glitter?"

I was annoyed with him for his flippant reaction to what I was really saying.

Of course I did wait and he did glitter. But it turned out that the lively beam of *his* success was not enough for me, though I was too young then to realize how important self-fulfillment was.

Learning to Be a Redgrave

Our weekends at Odiham were gala social events, and gastronomic delights played as important a role in Rachel's entertaining as in Vanessa's. But although I loved the house with its sweeping lawns and riotous abundance of English country flowers, I began quite early to feel that I didn't always want to attend the court of the Redgraves. If I voiced such an opinion, Corin was peeved. He was addicted to the routine of the Family Weekend. He insisted we spend our days off at one or another home, and so, of course, pay court we did.

It was on these weekends that I started to perceive how well the Redgraves played out the drama of The Family. The discussions were always scintillating—theater gossip, heated political discussions. They were all interested in each other's careers, without ever quite coming to grips with day-to-day life, with each other's personal problems or with any emotional crisis that might demand more than an outward show of affection. They would lavishly praise a performance, analyze each detail of Corin's makeup or delivery, but never noticed that our shoes were repaired with cardboard. I began to realize how impossible it was to ever think of bringing up the subject of our financial worries.

Like many of the people surrounding the Redgrave family circle, I was at first completely taken in by their image. It was very convincing. They played the close-knit theatrical family at home as well as they played Ibsen and Shakespeare on stage. Because I was unused to the flamboyance and constant parading, it took me a while to realize how far away my concept of real relationships was from theirs. Their world was made up of lines and gestures. When it came to practical proof of love, they seemed to lack the most basic consideration for each other.

Vanessa would sometimes ring up and invite Rachel enthusiastically for a meal, insisting that she missed her mother. But when Rachel arrived for dinner, beautifully dressed and full of anticipation, Vanessa wouldn't be there. She would either have forgotten completely or been called away to work and neglected to contact her mother.

They always seemed loving, kind, friendly . . . yet it was like a mirage, something there but not there.

Years later, having lived with them for so long, and in a way having become part of their lives and so part of the mirage itself, I began to realize how the very fact that they lived their lives almost constantly on stage or in the public eye imposed peculiar restrictions and obligations. Families like the Redgraves cannot let fly at one another in public without its being all over the papers the next day. They could not help but react to this. They felt there was an image to live up to, and since all were consummate actors, they did.

So they invented their own game, the game of being the perfect family, and the interrelationships between siblings and parents became like theater. They made up their own rules, and the result was an eternal production that closely resembled normal life but that I came to perceive as a fine facade.

I thought that through the Redgraves I had a new and valuable identity with name to match, that my married self would somehow be more rounded, more fascinating, more acceptable than my unmarried self. I was soon to be disillusioned, and it was Vanessa who unwittingly hacked at my new image until it began to crumble.

I had been to lunch with Vanessa and Tony about a dozen times when I registered that she had absolutely no idea who I was. She just managed to recall my name, but not once did she remember what I was doing or what were my interests in life.

One afternoon Corin and I were lunching at the house in Chiswick. When I heard my sister-in-law ask: "And what do *you* do?" for what seemed like the tenth time in as many weeks, I took my courage in both hands, glared at her wordlessly and stalked out of the room. Within seconds I had my coat in my hand and was dragging a bewildered Corin out into the autumn streets.

"What on earth's going on, Dee?" he asked, tugging at my recalcitrant elbow as I shuffled grumpily through the great crisp piles of dead leaves drifting across the pavement like spilled cornflakes.

"I can't stand your family," I snapped, smarting with hurt and humiliation. "Bloody snobbish cows. It's pretty damned obvious I don't mean anything in Vanessa's life, she doesn't even know who her brother's married to!"

"Don't be ridiculous," he said immediately, annoyed that I could be so childish. I was annoyed with myself too for letting them get to me.

"I'm sorry, Cor," I muttered. "It's just that she undermines me completely. We must have met forty, fifty, a hundred times by now—I don't know. All I know is that we see her for week-ends in the country, go to her plays, meet her for dinner, go to her house, spend hours at a time under the same roof—yet I might just as well be invisible. I doubt if she even knows my name. I just can't believe it! I don't know if she is evilly rude or pathologically absent-minded or if I am such a nothing person that I don't even register, even as her brother's wife!"

"Try to understand what it's like to be under the kind of pressure she's under all the time, Dee," he said. "She has an awful lot on her mind all the time—Sundays are her only days off— I'm really not surprised that she seems a bit thoughtless or forgetful sometimes but I'm also quite certain she doesn't realize she's upset you."

"I'm sure she doesn't," I retorted. "I'm sure by now she doesn't even remember I was there."

But Corin wouldn't be dragged into it any further. His face had the look of a man to whom the subject is closed. I did not add that his mother still expected me to call her Lady Redgrave.

In fact, it took Rachel nearly three years before it occurred to her to suggest I call her by her first name and drop the title.

Michael, I found, was not absent-minded so much as unapproachable. To catch him in a rare social situation was to find a man of ebullient wit and charm. To attempt to make contact at most other times was inadvisable unless you enjoyed bitter disappointments.

He was really almost a recluse.

In the months that followed our wedding day, I seldom saw

my father-in-law. He lived most of the time in his little studio at the end of the garden or was away in London when we visited Rachel and, after those first effusive displays of affection toward me upon my marriage to his son, was always very vague. But then he seemed hardly to know that his own children existed, so firmly did he set himself apart from the mainstream of daily life.

His children approached him with respect bordering on awe rather than with spontaneous love and warmth. I was used to treating my own father with a certain amount of diffidence and respect for his strength, position and age, but this was absurd. Although they never alluded to his almost unnatural reserve, I began to feel it was very hurtful for the children, especially Corin, who had needed a man to turn to. Michael had simply never been there for him.

If any of the children really reached their father it was probably Vanessa. Michael's firstborn held a special place in his heart, perhaps because she was the baby with whom he had spent the most time. The adulation was mutual. "I don't think there is an actor alive to touch my father," she would say. As time went on I began to feel an unvoiced sense of deprivation in the other two.

The Redgraves do not like headlong emotional confrontation. They do not like rows—they may use words to thrust and parry gently, but they will not argue in anger. It occurred to me that normal family conflict was sinister by its very absence.

8

Doubts

Although life as a Redgrave might not have been everything my fertile imagination had designed for me, it was still fun and full of surprises.

I can remember often answering the telephone at the cottage and finding one of my unreachable childhood heroines or heroes hanging on the end of the line. On one particular day it happened to be Scarlett O'Hara. Running in from the garden, brushing mud off my boots, I picked up the receiver and heard the most perfectly polished voice asking delicately to speak to Rachel. I suddenly realized it actually was Vivien Leigh.

Heart thudding, I expected her to launch into a sultry Southern accent and say, "Ashley, Ashley, I will love you forever"; I was immediately transported to Civil War days, into the arms of Clark Gable, and had changed my wellingtons for a low-cut velvet dress as Clark gazed down at me contemptuously saying, "Frankly, my dear, I don't give a damn!"

I was brought sharply back to earth by the sound of her abrupt and slightly surprised questioning in an extremely clipped upper-class accent. "This is the right number for Rachel Redgrave, isn't it? Would you please put me on to her at once? This is Lady Olivier."

Feeling firmly put in my place, Clark dissipating into thin air, muddy boots back solidly on my feet, I stammered my apologies and tramped through the kitchen to find Rachel, blushing at my own naiveté.

It was still difficult for me to come to terms with the fact that I was actually now an acceptable and accepted part of this exotic world where household names were, indeed, part of our household. There had really been nothing in my life so far, despite the smart convents and finishing schools, which had prepared me for bumping into my long-held fantasies in the flesh. Suddenly people who had lived for me only on the screen or on the stage were tangible parts of the life of my new family.

When Michael was in London working in a play, Rachel would often come up from the country, meet Corin and me at our flat, and we would all go on to collect Michael after the theater. Then he would take us out to elegant restaurants for dinner. One of his favorite places was the Grill at the Hyde Park Hotel, which had delicious food. The family had been known intimately there for years, so Michael was always given the best table—something the whole family took quite for granted.

Suddenly, instead of eating in little bistros with checked tablecloths where you brought your own wine, I found myself sailing into the most expensive restaurants in London on Corin's arm, being greeted by the maitre d'hotel and shown to the "Redgrave table" as though I were indeed entitled to this kind of attention.

It used to make me feel very conspicuous. Everyone would stare at us. In one way it made me feel like a goldfish in a bowl with the cats staring in, and in another way I really quite enjoyed it. My ego responded to the new-found flattery. It was a different reality from anything I'd known before, and occasionally I felt the two opposing reactions pulling me apart.

The Redgraves appeared to be completely unaware of the stir they caused. One night I was having dinner with Michael and Corin at the Savoy after attending an opening. Noël Coward was

On the island of Malta—Deirdre, her mother,
and her two brothers, Robert and Patrick.

Deirdre in 1959, at Cy Laurie's Jazz Club, a favorite
haunt for which she would abandon debutante balls.

The cottage at Odiham.

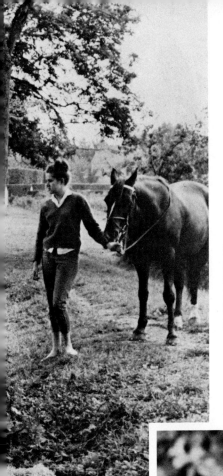

The Redgrave family in 1960, punting on the lake beside their country cottage at Odiham. Left to right: Corin, Lady Rachel, Vanessa, Sir Michael, and Lynn.

A publicity photo of Corin Redgrave early in his acting career.

Two sisters—Vanessa and Lynn.

Deirdre's wedding. Left to right: Corin, Deirdre, Sir Michael, Avril Vincent-Jones (bridesmaid), Lady Rachel, and Vanessa.

Reut

Two other stars of Deirdre and Corin's wedding—Vanessa and Sir Michael.

The Redgrave family at home. Standing, from left: Sir Michael Redgrave, Vanessa, Tony Richardson (Vanessa's husband), Lady Rachel Kempson. Kneeling: Lynn, Corin.

Portman Press Bureau Ltd.

Deirdre and Corin after their
wedding ceremony.

A prophetic coincidence—Corin
and Kika Markham, his present
girlfriend, after *their* wedding
ceremony in a television play, long
before Deirdre and Corin parted.

Beginning a family: Corin, Deirdre,
and infant Jemima in 1965.

Corin and Deirdre with daughter Jemma and son Luke, photographed with their fantasy Christmas presents: a harp for Corin, and a Harley-Davidson motorcycle for Deirdre.

Corin and Ben Arris on location for *The Charge of the Light Brigade*, 1967.

Deirdre and her children, Jemma and Luke.

The (London) *Times* Sunday Colour Supple

sitting at a nearby table, having attended the same event. Seeing Michael, he waved and immediately rose from his seat to cross the room to talk to us. You could physically feel the eyes of all the diners swivel in their sockets, following the distinguished figure as he threaded his way through the tables.

The name Noël Coward instantly conjured up a debonair, wise-cracking young blade with rapier wit. I was much too young to have ever actually seen him in *Blithe Spirit* or any of his other masterpieces. But in my childhood home, we had endless albums of Gertrude Lawrence and him performing their parts in *Private Lives*. Here was another living legend, reaching out a frail but surprisingly strong hand to take mine.

"My dear Michael, what an enchanting young woman, how lucky you are to have such a beautiful daughter-in-law."

As he looked at Corin and me with affection, it was some moments before I remembered I wasn't the witty Amanda of *Private Lives* swathed in floating chiffon, elegantly juggling two husbands by the light of the silvery moon.

When I looked again I saw an aging but extraordinarily distinguished gentleman exchanging words with one of his oldest friends. Both these magnificent actors seemed totally unaware of the effect they were having on the people around them, people with their very forks stopped in their tracks!

And, I couldn't help but notice, their gaze included *me*. It was at times like these that I was the most conflicted. I knew my looks and flair delighted my husband and almost made me feel a star—but it was not enough to justify my membership in this elevated circle. Whether it was due to guilt (I am here on false pretenses) or insecurity (I should *be* someone—not just someone's wife) or a just plain starving ego—I could not help thinking I had not quite undergone the true rites of passage necessary for inclusion.

I tried at least to look the part of a star. When I would appear with Corin, especially if I had taken the time and mustered the courage to dress up for the role of a glamorous lady of the theater, people would react. Sometimes it was really good fun. I would glide in on Corin's arm, sucking in my cheeks, pouting my lips in the best model's style of the time, wearing the shortest skirts in town and staring straight ahead disdainfully as though I had no idea that photographers were snapping my kneecaps and autograph books were being thrust under my upturned nose!

I was quickly learning my own brand of acting.

But sometimes I felt I couldn't pull it off, like the first time I actually met Vivien Leigh.

Corin and I were beginning to be part of what we called the "premiere belt"—invitations extended because we were "suitably qualified" to attend premieres, opening nights and cocktail parties to launch new plays. We would go, mostly because there was always free food, drink and tickets.

When we walked into the gracious high-ceilinged rooms of the Savoy, where a reception was being held for Vivien Leigh, I spotted her immediately, almost crushed in the melee of people all trying to reach her, talk to her, touch her.

"I can't," I said to Corin, panic-stricken, looking at the crowd.

"Nonsense," said Corin, grasping my sweaty hand firmly. "I'm going to steer you through all this and it'll be fine. I've known her all my life and she's dying to meet you. Don't be so silly, Dee. I didn't come all the way here for nothing."

So we bashed our way through the milling, shrieking party guests until we reached her table. I watched her for a while as Corin hovered, waiting for the right moment to introduce us.

Neat as a kitten, self-contained, tiny, unlined, bird-boned, she was a highly sophisticated woman of around fifty-five who looked fifteen years younger. Rachel had warned me that she had a fetish about her hands, thinking they were hideous, and always wore white gloves to cover them up. To me, the gloves simply added to the impression of delicacy. She was like a daisy or a magnolia blossom, its leaves faintly bruised by time but transparently beautiful still. Against her almost heartbreaking fragility I felt huge.

So I unconsciously bent down, trying to fold the frame of my own body to match hers, when suddenly Corin announced my presence and she turned from giving him a loving hug to embrace me too.

"Deirdre, my dear," she said, her voice existing in a perfect pool of stillness amid the babble. "I have been so looking forward to meeting you. Rachel tells me how beautiful you are, how happy you make dear Corin. I am so glad you are here. . . ."

Having rested her cheeks briefly against mine in that tangle of inebriated sophisticates of the theater, she stood back, extending her masked hand so regally that I had to catch myself from bending at the knee and kissing the fluttering fingers.

Afterward, when Corin and I were in bed that night talking about the party, I laughed and said, "What a wonderful performance." But the truth was that at the time I was quite overwhelmed by her presence. This tiny fragile woman could command a regiment, or so it seemed. And she had welcomed me with such charm, her polite peck on the cheek a sign of entry into her particular echelon of the acting aristocracy, that I could only feel glad.

Of course the pretty tricks of Scarlett had merged into mature grace, but the face looked almost the same. Her tragedies had not left her looking sour. Rachel had told me of how desperately unhappy Vivien had been when Sir Laurence abandoned her for the arms of a younger woman, actress Joan Plowright, whom he later married. But the great beauty betrayed none of the anger or insecurity that fading glory brings out in some women.

I reminded Corin of how, when his father was making a film with Bette Davis, Bette had been invited to lunch at Odiham, but had stipulated that "neither Lynn nor Vanessa be there." She confessed quite openly to Rachel her fear of female competition.

"I really don't like the comparison of sitting with younger women," was how Rachel relayed it, in perfect imitation of Bette's unique accents.

I remembered the things that one of my best friends, Trisha Locke, had told me. Trisha was living with Peter Finch at the time, and Peter had been one of the great loves of Vivien's life.

It did not threaten Trisha at all. It did not seem to threaten Vivien that Peter now lived with a much younger woman. Peter and Trisha were often invited to stay at Vivien's home, and Trisha always enjoyed herself thoroughly.

She told me how Vivien and Peter still had a secret lovers' signal for when they wanted to make contact with one another in a room full of people. They would look up to the ceiling and down again, rapidly.

Trisha said that the reason she never felt any fear or jealousy of Vivien was because there was a mystical quality to the love Peter and Vivien shared, an intangible, surreal quality which set it apart from daily lives, and daily living was what Trisha shared with Peter. It was tacitly agreed by both women that neither would encroach upon the territory of the other.

Corin and I also became intensely involved in the gambling scene just beginning to take hold in London. After Corin had finished working at the theater, and I had changed from my striped apron, checked shirt, and blue jeans waitress's uniform into something more glamorous, we would head for a gambling club in Knightsbridge called Esmerelda's Barn. It was owned by the Kray twins, the now notorious East End criminals, and was frequented by the young elite of London. We became hooked on chemin de fer. Or at least I did. I was always more reckless and didn't take losing as badly as Corin.

We had an account with a bookmaker and were generally lucky on the horses, but at the chemmy table we risked more—it was more dangerous and more exciting. We were sufficiently badly off for the turn of a card, the right card, to mean a treat, a romantic dinner, new shoes, even a holiday, but we could not afford to lose.

One evening everything seemed to be in our favor. We couldn't lose. Every gambler knows that feeling, the lucky streak. You feel enchanted; you know you cannot put a foot down wrong; fate is on your side. We sat at the green baize table, stacking up chips into a pile in front of us. The air was full of smoke; in the background we heard the whipping of the roulette wheel and the click of the little ball slotting into a number and color that would create happiness or despair for those crowded around the table. The croupier's words, *Mesdames et Messieurs, rien ne va plus*, rang in our ears.

As the pile of chips increased in size and the croupier pushed more and more of the plastic chips in our direction, other people began to watch us and follow our moves. It was exhilarating. I was flying high and could have stayed all night, but Corin was more sensible than I.

"Come on, we're going while we are up," he said firmly, not listening to my "Oh buts" and "Just a little longer." The good wife in me meekly said yes, so we wandered home, walking briskly through the chill spring night, dazed at our good fortune.

The following morning we rose early and went on a shopping spree. Money won gambling burns a hole in the pocket—it demands to be spent, and we spent it. New shoes, new coats, a new wardrobe and a large, delicious lunch to celebrate.

When Corin returned from the theater that night, I, still high, persuaded him, much against his better judgment to go again. We had a little change left from our shopping spree, and if our luck held out, Esmerelda's Barn seemed a sound investment.

Once again we walked into the smoke-filled atmosphere, ordered our drinks and took our places at the oval table. But this time the feeling was decidedly different. In no time at all our small pile of chips had disappeared. Corin went to buy some more. We lost over and over again, desperately chasing our losses, until this time I was the one who decided we should leave. We walked home once more through the streets of Knightsbridge, this time dejectedly.

Corin was white with fury. Throwing money away on cards was madness to him. I knew it was my fault, and I didn't dare speak. I was always frightened of him when he was in such a mood. We arrived home in silence, went to bed in silence, woke up in silence, and he had not said one word to me when he left for his matinee.

I could not think of a way to appease him. Our financial problems were such that the amount of money we had lost would weigh on his mind forever, and I knew that, really, the trips to Esmerelda's Barn were always much more exciting for me than for him. I decided to risk everything. I rang an old friend, asked him to stake me, assuring him that I had family jewelry sufficient to pay him back if I lost.

First we went to dinner at the White City dog-racing track where I backed a few winners, and, with growing confidence, we went to Crockford's, where I would try my luck once more. And lucky I was! Once again, the magic feeling—I could not go wrong. Suddenly I realized it was three o'clock in the morning. I had never been out before when Corin returned from the theater; I had left no note. What he must be thinking! I thanked my friend, cashed in my chips, and, stuffing the notes in my handbag, rang for a taxi. I reached home petrified. Perhaps he wouldn't even be there. Hoping he might be asleep, I took my shoes off and crept into the darkened flat. Corin was most definitely awake. He was sitting, still the same look of fury he had worn last night on his face, slouched in an armchair.

"Where the hell have you been?" he demanded.

I opened my handbag and threw the money at him. It swirled around his head like confetti.

"I hope that makes you happy," I cried and ran into the bedroom. He followed me.

"Are you all right, Dee?" he asked, concerned. "I've been so worried about you, please, please, never do anything like that again." He was almost stammering. "I thought you might have left me."

I was so relieved I leaped from the bed where I'd thrown myself in fury and jumped instead upon Corin. Hugging him and kissing him as hard as I could, I babbled on about how I didn't mean to worry him, but that I couldn't bear it when he froze me out with those terrible silences. And how all I wanted to do was to make the money back again for us, because it was all my fault we lost in the first place.

Doubts

Each day I learned more about how differently we expressed our emotions. My feelings rise quickly to the surface, are obvious to anyone who cares to look. My face gives it all away. Corin's are buried deep. If I am a volcano, then he is an iceberg, with seven-eighths of his emotional life below the surface.

Perhaps it was one of the reasons we were so drawn to each other in the first place. He to my openness and warmth; me to his icy depths.

I learned never to expect great displays of any feeling from him. Although I understood that after a while the delirium of ecstasy settles into comfortable closeness—and our physical life was affectionate—I felt that Corin was somehow always holding himself aloof. Even at intimate moments, he never quite dropped that mysterious guard which I tried to penetrate and failed.

But outwardly he did change. When we first met he never wanted to go out dancing and would only go to clubs if I dragged him there, and then only on very special occasions. Now he actually suggested the idea himself from time to time. It was quite a change from his almost fanatical dedication to books and endless study, and I was delighted. More and more often he would take my arm when we walked in the street, leave little notes for me to find when he had gone to work, and would shyly search for my fingertips in the cinema, or bring me back flowers, if there was ever any extra money.

As it is for all couples, this year was a period of adjustment for us. We were learning to make space for one another's eccentricities, habits, wishes and desires.

But as our everyday routines continued (Corin leaving for the theater, me for my job at the restaurant), I became aware of an uncomfortable feeling of emptiness. Our house seemed unnaturally quiet to me—my parents' house was always filled with people, and the flats I had shared with friends had rocked with chaos and laughter. And I felt a void inside. I didn't know whether the feeling stemmed from my marriage or if it was emptiness in myself. I just felt an undefined discontent—and I had no outlet for it. Corin had a career, or a choice of careers, and was heading toward something. I could not see myself heading toward anything.

It is hard to believe now that I had so little motivation of my own. But I was not ambitious. I had no desire to be a star of anything myself. My adolescent dreams were invested in marriage, and I was afraid to step outside it—fearful that this would separate me from Corin, unsure of anything but my ability to be a wife, and maybe a mother.

Perhaps if I had had a keener sense of competition or ambition, our lives would never have become as polarized as they did. If I were to run back the reel and have that time again, it would be crucially different. I would work seriously at a career. I have discovered over the years that I enjoy having one. I like the feeling of satisfaction that comes with hard work and achievement outside the home. I had no idea at that time that people become infinitely more fascinating to one another if they have a world apart and can bring its secrets and joys into their world shared.

I thought there was no solution to the sense of married loneliness that I was experiencing other than having a child. I wondered whether motherhood would provide a purpose for me in life more than simply helping to support my husband.

It was toward the end of this first year that I began to peer surreptitiously into prams as they passed me in the street with their tiny swaddled cargo.

9

Manhattan Transfer

"We must go!" Corin said excitedly one evening while we were dressing to go out, he to the theater, me to my job. "The play's going to America and they want me to go too. *Chips with Everything* certainly seems to be a part of our life—we've courted through it, married during it—can you face it being the backdrop to your first visit to America as well?"

He turned to me, smiling, watching for my reaction, looking back to the mirror to knot the tie before slipping on his jacket. I had not seen him so enthusiastic in ages. I thought he was getting bored with the play. But America! America was a change, a challenge, and I knew he loved challenges.

"Of course I can face it!" I said, putting my arms around him, hugging him from behind and meeting his bright blue dancing eyes in the mirror. "I can't wait to see the States. If we go there with the play then they'll pay for your ticket, we'll know that we have money when we get there—you'll become a Broadway star!"

Best of all, we could explore the unknown territory together. It was time for us to have an adventure, to shake up our lives a little, to find new input and excitement. When Corin is interested in something, his anticipation is catching.

"What shall I do?" I queried laughingly. "Start packing now?"

"Soon," said Corin, patting my bottom. And sure enough, in about a month's time I was getting us ready for our great new venture across the water.

It was 1963—the year of the British invasion of America. The Beatles were making rock history by drawing in vast audiences of young people and turning the airways inside out with Beatlemania, open references to drugs, and their crazy Liverpudlian sense of humor. Mary Quant presented young British fashion to America, and young America went wild for microskirts, Sassoon squared haircuts and pale lipstick. By 1964 there were eight successful British plays on Broadway and *Chips with Everything* was one of them.

My husband's decision to go with it to America was partly based on the irresistible lure of the unknown, partly on a desire to investigate his chances in the film world—of which America was the undisputed heart. Vanessa and Lynn had not yet made their indelible imprint on the movie screens. But Michael had been lionized by Hollywood, where he had been making films successfully for many years, and Corin was drawn to the arena, feeling that with his exposure on Broadway, film success couldn't be far behind.

I had to admit that Corin's track record so far had been less than brilliant. The only film he had made in Britain was a disastrously unfunny comedy called *Crooks in the Cloister*, with Francesca Annis, which was instantly forgotten. Still we felt that given the right director, the right script, the right chance, his presence on stage would be more than equaled by his presence on screen.

It was far more important to Corin, a perfectionist, that he find the right role, the right niche, than it was to achieve instant fame and fortune. He would accept a continuation of his part in *Chips with Everything* because it was a well-written role that he knew he performed well. He considered it a production of integrity. This was essential. I knew my husband well enough by now to know that there was no way he could be bribed by the tinsel promises of superficial success.

Corin went first. For one thing he did not mind flying, and I did. For another we had to wind up our affairs in London, and the only way we could balance our budget was to let our flat in Kensington while we were away. Since there was an element of doubt still hanging over the entire venture, Corin sensibly insisted we at least wait to find out whether the play would survive the critics.

But it did. Not only did it survive, but our nights of nail-biting anxiety were over: it was a roaring success. The first letter I had from Corin allayed all my fears; he wrote of an extraordinary premiere, including a standing ovation, and being feted at parties where the guests included Tony Perkins, Tony Curtis, Peter Sellers and James Baldwin. He asked me to come quickly so that we could share the New York adventure. Within days I had rented the flat and was on my way to Manhattan by ship. A lashing hurricane slowed down the journey, and we were days late arriving in New York. But it didn't matter. It was a clear, crisp, sunny autumn morning, and at least we were there and alive and well.

Manhattan appeared slowly over the horizon. Because of the Cuban crisis, I was sharply aware of the possibility of nuclear war. As the ship drew nearer the city, and the great skyscrapers loomed large against the pure horizon, they seemed to be tempting the gods to destroy them.

I stood with my elbows on the cold steel of the railings, glad to see Manhattan first from the sea—an extraordinary and beautiful sight. But the beauty seemed to be tinged with arrogant folly; the concentration of materialism on one tiny island was a symbol invoking disaster.

My fellow passengers and I waved happily to the Statue of Liberty and then spent hours waiting to disembark; people pushing and pulling their way through Customs and Immigration. I looked down for Corin's familiar figure but couldn't see him anywhere. Because of the change in schedule caused by the hurricane, he was doing a matinee while I was setting foot on American soil for the first time in my life.

I heard an American voice say "Hi" in a warm and intimate way. I turned instinctively as though my best friend were at my elbow. It was Corin's American agent, who would take me to my new home—I was to meet Corin at the theater. He took me from the dock to our apartment. We tore past SoHo with its forbidding warehouses and desolate streets. By the time we passed the Chelsea Hotel, which even I had heard of, the houses were smaller and neater, and where I had imagined vast skyscrapers jamming every street of New York, here we were right in the middle of what seemed like a small town.

In fact, the area was called Chelsea. Our apartment was on Twenty-second Street, between Ninth and Tenth Avenues, a small four-story brownstone. We had the top floor. No tubular steel and modern paintings. I had always thought that shiny plastic and the hard sharp lines of streamlined architecture were synonymous with America, especially Manhattan. But this was a home full of beautiful antiques and polished wood, and, at the very heart of it, a log fire blazed, a symbol of reassurance.

I unpacked and decided to put on my finest London gear. Since Corin had signed the new contract for America, our financial situation had improved. Short skirts and trouser suits and beautiful printed chiffon scarves filled my wardrobe, and Rachel, as a generous going-away present, had bought me a striking Mary Quant evening coat that I'd coveted for months. I chose Corin's favorite outfit, a black trouser suit—he loved me in black, said it made me look more dramatic.

So, decked out to the nines, I ventured out by myself into the streets of New York for the first time. Although I'd heard terrible stories about people being beaten up and had been told that women should never go out alone, I was far too excited to find it threatening.

"Would you take me to Broadway, please?" I asked the taxi driver.

"Sure, lady," he said. "I guess you want that new English play?" And to my amazement he launched into a long critique of *Chips with Everything*. I was later to discover that among the most reliable sources of information on new cultural events in theater, cinema and art are the New York City cabdrivers.

Of course the driver knew exactly where the theater was, as well as the stage door, where my name had been left with the doorman, and I was quickly shown the way to Corin's dressing room.

As I walked through the maze of little corridors behind the stage I could hear great rolls of thunderous applause ricocheting around the theater. The sound of success. I sat waiting for Corin in his dressing room, and he came running in the moment he could get off the stage, grabbed me in his arms and plastered pancake all over my carefully made up face and pristinely new suit. It was wonderful.

My first evening in New York had already been planned. Corin took me to Sardi's, the famous theatrical restaurant. We were shown to our table with a flourish by the maitre d'hotel, who knew Corin's face well. He was in a smash hit, and that makes all the difference in the way waiters treat actors. Until now it had always been Michael who commanded the instant respect of doormen, servants and waiters. Now at last it was Corin himself. I knew that he had earned that respect on his own terms, and that it pleased him. It pleased me to see the new pride in his bearing that might not be apparent to others, but was to me. I felt extraordinarily happy and proud of him. It was time for him to bask in his own limelight, and time for me to share it with him.

He held my hand under the table with its elaborate silver and bowl of roses and ordered a bottle of the best champagne, always our choice when we wanted to give ourselves a treat. I looked around for the first time at the other people in the restaurant.

Sitting in a corner was the dapper figure of Rex Harrison, then married to Rachel Roberts. Rex was an old friend of Michael's and had known Corin since childhood. Not long before, the two of them had worked together in a play at the Royal Court when Corin was acting as well as trying stage management. He wanted to learn all aspects of theater, and at first was as much interested in becoming a director as he was in becoming an actor. Tony Richardson persuaded him to choose the stage.

Corin told me he used to hear Rex's lines for him when they were working together. "We would go over them again and again. I think he must be one of the most meticulous actors I've ever worked with."

Although his hair was graying, and the somewhat sardonic face was creased with lines of humor and life, Rex still had the dashing air of a gentleman pirate. Before they left, he and Rachel came over to speak to us and congratulate Corin.

"You'll adore New York, darling," said Rachel to me in her throaty voice. And she was right. I did. For if you are in a successful box-office hit in New York you are made—at least for the play's duration. We were feted and courted and wined and dined and taken everywhere that was anywhere—the other kinds of places we discovered for ourselves.

To add to the festivities, Tony Richardson arrived in New York to direct the Tennessee Williams play *The Milk Train Doesn't Stop Here Anymore*. He had cast Tallulah Bankhead as the predatory old woman, Mrs. Goforth, and Tab Hunter as the seductively youthful Angel of Death. He took an enormous gamble by starring the unpredictable Tallulah, playing her decadent, aging charms against the almost inane glamour of surfing-boy Tab.

When Tony invited me to meet them both in the mahogany-lined dining room of the Algonquin Hotel, I was struck most forcibly not by her famous husky, haunting voice, nor by her legendary beauty, but by her hands, which had been burned to the bone by forgotten cigarettes. Tony told me she was an alcoholic and addicted to nicotine. Those holes in her skin were from fag ends which had burned their way permanently into flesh numbed by gin. The scars could not be disguised.

Tab Hunter, on the other hand, was as wholesome as a glass of milk. And as interesting. He said little, and I was forcibly reminded of the song "New York Is a Lonely Town When You're the Only Surfing Boy Around."

"How," I asked Tony sardonically, "could Tallulah ever compete with Annette Funicello?"

It remained to be seen whether Tony could put these two polar opposites together on one stage and come up with something dynamic.

Tony escorted me to the opening night. We entered the theater in a state of near panic, and we left halfway through to tear around the corner to the nearest bar to stoke up with some alcoholic fuel, returning just in time to find an audience torn between admiration and incomprehension.

(Tennessee Williams was later to discuss this production in his book *Memoirs*. He was clearly enthusiastic about the casting of Tallulah, but Williams's dry observation of Tab Hunter as the Angel of Death was that Tony must have "owed Tab a favor or two." Tallulah, when asked whether she thought Tab was gay or not, apparently replied with her usual acerbic wit, "I don't know. I haven't fucked him.")

One member of the cast, a good friend of Tony's, was another legendary American actress, Ruth Gordon, wife of writer Garson Kanin. She took an instant shine to Corin and me and swept us under her wing in an almost maternal way, making us feel at home in her vast apartment in the exclusive Dakota apartment house and regularly inviting us to parties.

But we also managed to break away from this absurdly rarefied atmosphere. Every Thursday night, teams from the eight British plays on Broadway would compete with each other in bowling. After the show, we would all go to Times Square, munch on some pizzas, swig wine and head for the bowling alley, where we would either dislocate our elbows bowling or make ourselves hoarse by cheering our teams.

But I inevitably spent a great deal of time on my own, while Corin was at the theater. Since I was not working, there were hours and days in which to explore the city, and I began to find its social polarities disturbing. I would turn down one fashionable street to find the most extreme poverty on the next. Walking down Fifth Avenue I would frequently be confronted by beggars. I would sit on the subway and watch the all-pervading helplessness which showed itself at night, in the poor districts, in the subway, on Forty-second Street and on the Lower East Side.

It seemed extraordinary that only a short distance from the extreme riches and elegance of Park Avenue with all its shops and elaborate archaic hotels was the Bowery, where hundreds lay prostrate on the streets, uncared for, uncaring, seeking only the oblivion they could find in a bottle of alcohol.

And the racism shocked me. In England I had not experienced black antagonism, or the reasons for it. Nor had I witnessed that turbulent division between white and black which was just beginning to clash in middle-class America.

Both Corin and I wanted to see Harlem. I wanted to go to the Apollo Theater to make a pilgrimage to the roots of rock and roll. I remembered that Buddy Holly was the first white musician to play there, and Aretha Franklin, B. B. King, Billie Holliday and James Brown had sanctified its stage with their songs and sweat. The names of the master musicians streamed past my consciousness, and I wanted to see it for myself. But none of our black friends in New York would go with us. They implied it was much too dangerous either for whites to go alone or for blacks to go with whites. They would incur the anger of their brothers.

We could not understand their paranoia. At that stage we had no comprehension of the seriousness of the problem. We made up our minds that we would go, guides or no guides, even if it meant seeing everything from the inside of a yellow cab.

We hailed one in the Village. When the driver learned we wanted to go through Harlem, his face closed. Eventually he agreed to take us, but only on his conditions.

"Make sure your doors are locked," he said. "That's in case of trouble at traffic lights. Then you gotta guarantee to keep your windows wound up and leave it to me to choose the route."

That seemed fair enough, so we agreed and bundled ourselves

into the taxi, our anticipation sharpened by curiosity and a quick weasel's nip of fear at the bottom of the gut.

Once we emerged from the fancy houses of the Upper East Side, the streets began to reflect incredible poverty and dilapidation. House after house had been burned down. Windows were smashed in, leaving gaping holes. On street corners bitter down-at-the-heels youths gathered in surly gangs. Sometimes an angry face pressed against the car window. Old men in battered narrow-brimmed hats sucked on curved pipes and old women in curlers trundled down the pavements with their shopping bags.

Even the young girls looked old. Old with poverty and pain. Some of them had babies in derelict prams, or carried them on their backs, the babies' tiny bare feet often sticking out in the cold wind.

There was an air of suppressed resentment and lethal subversion, which we could feel even through the locked doors and windows.

We understood finally that there was a real barrier between the black and white districts of New York. It might be invisible but that did not mean that there was anything other than a taut wire of tension on which either side could cut itself to ribbons.

We held hands as the cab sped back to the rich areas of the city. We both felt guilty at our own comfort. As though we were looking at other people's hardships from the luxurious vantage point of a traveler, an observer. We didn't want to be observers; we wanted to be involved. Really involved. To improve the situation. We were both so emotionally distraught by what we had seen that I think now it might well have been the single most important factor which precipitated our later involvement with minority causes and, most crucially, with the Black Power movement as it spread to Britain.

It wasn't as though we hadn't experienced our own brand of bigotry in Europe. Even on my beloved island of Malta I had encountered racism against the beautiful native people whose country it really was.

But New York was polarized. The differences were drawn in blood. The oppressed cried out for freedom and the oppressors cried out in fear. This we had seen. Until that trip our only knowledge of the black culture of the country was through people who were for the most part actors or musicians, people who, via art or entertainment, had broken the color bar to white acceptance. Barriers of skin, class and creed exist far less among artists than among any other kinds of people.

The passion of black people in England at that time was much less raw to the eye than the growing anger of blacks in America. Europeanized blacks had a patina of cosmopolitan sophistication which often cloaked and disguised their real feelings. I don't think either Corin or I had the faintest idea of the real feelings of black minorities until we went to America. Going into Harlem showed us people who wore no cloaks.

Corin and I were lying lazily in bed one afternoon when an actor friend telephoned us to turn on the television, that something really awful was happening in Dallas.

Like everyone else in America, we switched on the television and, to our horror, watched the entire bloody tragedy played out before our eyes. We watched the car carrying the President's body racing for the hospital. We saw frantic crowds jostling and fighting each other for a better look at their dying President. Finally a weeping announcer informed the nation that Kennedy had died.

We were totally stunned. Speechless.

The assassination of one of America's most charismatic Presidents was at that moment written in indelible ink on the minds of the American people. And on ours, too; we would never forget. For the first time in history, Broadway's Great White Way was darkened, and the show did not go on. Corin and I walked hand in hand, numbed, through the streets of New York, as traumatized by the appalling suddenness of what had happened as all the other people we saw aimlessly wandering through Manhattan.

The golden boy of politics had been gunned down in broad daylight, annihilated by the very weapons he sought to restrict. If it could happen to him it could happen to anyone here. And did. His brother Robert, Martin Luther King, Malcolm X, . . . the list goes on, will go on. Perhaps even John Lennon's fate was already sealed in a gunshot.

It sent shivers up my spine. Not for the first time the hot angry violence of the city struck me with arrows as I looked down on it from my half-opened window. It came to me that it was time for us to go home.

Corin's run ended in the late spring of 1964. Together we decided not to stay. New York had been a rough, tough injection of pure energy into our veins. But there was too much troubled, churning malevolence—the threats of violence were too imminent for comfort. We needed time to sort out what we had learned. Neither of us chose to do that in America. Home and the tranquil fields of England beckoned like a paradise. It was with relief that we found ourselves on a boat headed back to Southampton and what we imagined would be peace and harmony.

✥ 10 ✥

Second Honeymoon

A holiday in Malta seemed the perfect answer. Relieved to be back but exhausted from the five-month American experience, we both decided to take a break.

My family still lived on the island. When my father first went there, when I was seven, as Director of Rediffusion, he was effectively in command of the island media. Years later he introduced television to Malta. It was a job for which he was later to earn the Order of the British Empire, for services rendered in the interest of the Crown.

My mother and I had followed my father there by troop ship in 1946. The boat was so crowded with passengers that we were like sardines packed in olive oil. I remember heaving seas and garlic breath, and a gnawing apprehension. It was hard to believe this was to be my home, this strange little island right in the middle of the Mediterranean. We anchored in the ancient harbor of Valletta, its capital, famed for the beautiful forts and battlements that surrounded it, carved out of honey-gold stone and bathed in sunlight. As the boat steamed in, I gazed over the railings, astonished at this alien land.

Second Honeymoon

Valletta was silent in the middle of the day. Siesta time. The architecture was foreign and remote, the heat oppressive. A launch chugged its way slowly across the water bearing a stranger called my father. For the first seven years of my life I had barely seen him. I started crying and begged to be allowed to return to England, to the friends I had made. This new landscape seemed impenetrable, unfriendly and threatening.

But it changed into a love affair. I still consider Malta my home. My first home. My soul home. I miss the feel of the hot sun on my skin, burning sand under my feet, the song of the crickets, golden sun heating golden stone, diving into turquoise water, swimming down to the sand and seaweed and the mystery of the dark life of the ocean.

I became enamored of a race so ancient that its foundations are in the culture of the Phoenicians, who were the first to discover it in their sea quests. Many invasions from different countries followed, from the Turks through to the Arabs and Moors, until finally the British, who were invited there to help rid the island of the French. The Maltese people are renowned for their sense of humor: when dealing with so many pretenders to their throne, it was certainly a necessity.

Often, as I trudged through the wet streets of London, struggling with horrible plastic bags filled with food from the supermarket, icy wind chilling my bones, I mourned the sun-spilled streets of that tiny island. I wanted Corin to know about the time in my life when I ran barefoot on warm pavements, lived in the sea in the daytime, stayed up late into long summer nights. My brothers and I became Mediterranean. I'm sure the warm, exotic environment helped shape our personalities.

I told him also of less happy memories. I told him how it was my first intimation of racism, after which I began to identify more and more with the Maltese people, learning their language, one of the oldest known to man, and learning their customs. I was also learning to identify with oppressed people.

Corin could understand that. He and Vanessa were already

public in their political commitments. The Left held sway in their lives, even if their campaigns for the politically and socially oppressed had not yet begun in earnest.

Corin and I arrived on the island in late spring. My mother and father met us at the airport and drove us home through the sunbaked streets. As I watched my husband's face I could see a reflection of my own first doubts. The streets were narrow and winding and difficult to negotiate. Washing hung in colored strips from crumbling balconies. Old women shouted to each other on street corners. There was no trace of greenery to be seen. No palm trees, no oleanders, no bougainvillea until one reached the country.

Corin's face was tightening before my eyes. I knew that closed look. It was the one he reserved for cutting off emotional outbursts and condemning those things or people of which he disapproved. I dreaded it.

"Don't make judgments yet, Cor," I whispered and squeezed his hand. "Wait and see, wait and you'll see the beauty. It took me time too, to find it. Let me show you what I know."

Finally we drew up to the house. It was as beautiful as always, full of flowers, soft lights and the inviting smell of fresh herbs. Something like Odiham. I could see Corin physically relax. By the time we had been shown to our room, had unpacked, showered, dressed for dinner, Corin was happy, and I had found again the warm playground of my childhood.

My brothers, Robert and Patrick, came rushing into our room to greet us. They were on holiday from their public schools in England and wanted to get to know, or rather to torment in natural, healthy rivalry, their new brother-in-law. They dragged us downstairs and into the dining room, impatient for their meal.

"You both look half-starved," said my mother. "Didn't you eat anything while you were in America? By the time you leave here you'll be brown and have some flesh on your bones. I'll make sure of that."

"But I don't want flesh on my bones, Mum," I said irritated, beginning immediately to feel like a child again. "I work hard not to have any."

"Your mother is perfectly right," said Corin. "If I'd wanted to marry a skinny model, I'd have done so."

The conversation continued for some time with me as the center of criticism. I was used to being treated like a child by my family, but I was not used to it from Corin and I didn't like it at all. I wanted support from him. This was the first time he had been in *my* home, although I had been in his many times.

It wasn't just that I wanted to show him everything I knew and loved and had held dear for so long despite my distance from it. But also that I wanted to show *him* off, as my knight in shining armor. I wanted my family to see him support me and love me. Instead I felt inexplicably brought down. I felt that in his eyes I was as much a child as I was in the eyes of my parents. I wanted to appear to them now as a poised and beautiful woman, secure in her happy marriage to a poised and beautiful man. In reality it was difficult to maintain my dignity.

Later, in the privacy of our bedroom, Corin asked why I had become so annoyed earlier, and I attempted to explain my feelings. He did not begin to comprehend what I was talking about and again made me feel silly and overemotional. I wanted to take him the next day to the first convent school I ever attended. The evening had made me slightly nervous that he wouldn't take that seriously, either.

The day dawned as miraculously blue and gold as I had hoped. "Let's go to the chapel where I used to pray when I was a little girl," I urged Corin. "It really would mean a lot if you'd come with me."

I knew that Corin's philosophies were already veering toward Marx, although not yet defined or labeled as such. Religion or spiritual experience had never at any point made up the fabric of his life. He tolerated my rather haphazard and irregular adherence to the Christian faith but did not encourage it or make much effort to understand how I felt about God. He simply never thought about theology.

But this time he agreed to come with me. I introduced him to the gentle nuns with smiling wrinkled faces who had known me since childhood and extended their pale veined hands to greet my husband. He was fastidiously polite to the women who were my first teachers, asked them smiling pertinent questions, wandered thoughtfully through the cool cloisters of my youth and revealed nothing of his atheism.

I was more than relieved. I linked fingers with him and walked toward the peaceful chapel. He would not come in, so I left him outside in the warm sunlight and entered the shadowy room, so full of memories and sweet familiar smells of incense. I knelt and prayed. I thought about who I was now. I was not a child any more. I wore high heels and lipstick and had a man at my side. I couldn't swing on the swings. I was too old to fling my arms around my favorite nuns. I was a woman who had trod in women's ways. I wondered if I would have been happier had I joined the cloistered life of denial and self-sacrifice. As I clasped my hands together, I prayed that wherever my choices had led me and would lead me, it would be with the blessings of the Church.

When I left the chapel's shade for the midday heat, it was with a feeling of calm. It had been a while since I had been to church; somehow, living with an atheist had nudged me away from the habit of going regularly. Now I felt pleasantly at peace. I smiled at Corin, and he smiled sweetly back.

But he is a consummate actor. I had forgotten. The moment we were down the driveway and out of sight of the nuns, his composed bearing changed to a gasp of hilarity.

"My dear Dee!" he exclaimed. "How can you take all that crap seriously?"

I was aghast, desolate.

"What happened, darling?" He was laughing uncontrollably by now, and I was livid. "Did you have a vision in the chapel? Did you perhaps talk to the Virgin Mary who was the Mother of Christ but still a virgin? Do you now wish that you too had chosen a life of endless piety?"

He had an uncanny knack for exactly hitting a sensitive spot.

He knew well that I had fleetingly considered a simple and spiritually rewarding religious life, and for perhaps the first time in our relationship I realized that Corin had a streak of cruel cynicism unmatched in anyone else I had ever met.

Yet however deep his distaste for religion and for the Roman Catholic Church in particular, I did not expect such an attack on what had obviously moved me. He dismissed all organized religions as tools used by those in power to subjugate others and promote the class system. Over the years I was to find that he never acknowledged the core of me that I called "faith." I found that his attitude undermined my own beliefs, cast doubts on my intelligence and allowed me no sense of who I was.

Within years he had washed away my faith in the answers of the Catholic Church to the eternal questions of life, my faith in spirit and soul, in redemption and reincarnation. He did not believe in life after death and did not want me to.

I had never expected to change the convictions Corin had held all his life. At the time I believed him—or wanted to. Corin and my marriage became my faith—until the day I found I could believe in him, and in it, no longer.

I never told him any of this. I found it difficult to talk to my husband about the things that mattered most to my heart.

By mutual consent, the rest of the holiday was lived out on a physical plane; the metaphysical was left alone. We went swimming, diving, riding, water skiing, sailing, and played tennis with my younger brothers. Singles Corin invariably won. Doubles, with me, were an inevitable loss, and he was inconsolable.

But I took him down the winding road to the port and sat him down at a street café for a glass of Marsovin, the amber liquid which was the local wine. We made up our differences. We would watch the sunset quietly and hold hands lightly. If my parents persuaded us to dine at home, it was on grilled prawns in garlic sauce. If we drank with them at the end of the day, it was their favorite Pimm's Number Two, decorated with sugar frosting and slices of fruit and cucumber, in the best colonial tradition.

The two of us established a soft, sensual rapport that we often lost in London, where city life interferes with personal contact. Corin and I spent more time than usual in bed. I would wake in the morning with Corin's arms still wrapped around me. And sometimes in the moonlight, I remembered about the island's fertility spell.

It was time to start a family of my own. I surprised myself. But I wanted Corin and me to be closer, I wanted a positive outlet for my energy, and I fell into believing that a new life will bind an old one together.

I began to suspect I was pregnant as we prepared for our journey home. I was twenty-five. "Time," I said to Corin, "for the next step."

I was right.

11

New Life, New Love

Time, and the gradual but perceptible changes in my body that were concrete evidence of new life inside me, helped me accustom myself to the strangeness of first pregnancy. I began to feel a sense of private fulfillment. Instead of feeling lonely and neglected when the door slammed as Corin left for the theater every evening, I was quite happy to spend alone those hours he was away. I felt that because I was nurturing a baby inside me I had a purpose. There was a real meaning to life, a definite sense of fulfilling time-honored tradition, of the rightness of bearing my husband's child, of embarking on the adventure of creating a new family.

The pre-London tour of Corin's new play, *The Right Honorable Gentleman*, with Anna Massey, Coral Browne and Anthony Quayle, had been a success, and their West End run looked set to be a long one. We were still living comfortably in the flat in Gloucester Road so at least we had a roof over our head and some of my fears about money were allayed.

It was 1964. I never felt I had a choice as to whether or not I should eventually have children. It was just part of the business of being a woman. The idea of putting a career before having a baby because a baby might curtail my freedom simply never occurred. Morning sickness, swollen ankles, tiredness and general discomfort notwithstanding, I found pregnancy more fascinating than irritating.

So did Corin. He became overwhelmingly romantic and sentimental. He told me he thought I looked beautiful. He plied me with flowers, rubbed oil on my belly, and sang to me the song from *Carousel* celebrating the birth of a child, be it little boy or little girl.

We didn't care what sex our child was. Corny as the most sentimental song, and silly as teenagers, we'd put our arms around each other and sing together boisterously, turning our living room into a stage. We were entranced by the very idea of our child, besotted by the vista of parenthood stretching before us.

As though to add to our pleasure, we learned that Vanessa was pregnant with her second child, and our babies were due at the same time, around the beginning of January 1965.

Vanessa and Tony already had one daughter, Natasha, born the year before, so Vee was well equipped to initiate me into the secrets of pregnancy and childbirth. She and I grew much closer as our pregnancies progressed. We would spend long lazy afternoons together, chatting and exchanging information as friends. For the first time we were more than just sisters-in-law, we were women friends, sharing the bond of expectant motherhood.

Vee had been to natural childbirth classes when she was expecting Natasha. She strongly recommended this method of giving birth, using a version of the Lamaze method of breathing so that fewer drugs and less medical interference were needed during labor. As Vee described the amazing feeling of satisfaction she had at being conscious during Natasha's birth, I realized that I wanted mine to be as natural as possible too.

She urged me to go to relaxation classes. I discovered the National Childbirth Trust and learned the same kind of breathing Vee already knew and practiced.

I also went through a phase—perhaps all mothers do—of feeling that maybe I shouldn't have the baby. Because someone had invented the nuclear bomb, Hiroshima had happened and might again, Cuba and the Cold War had already almost crippled our society, and the American invasion of Vietnam was accelerating, I wondered how safe or sage a world we had and was worried by the madness into which I might be bringing my baby.

Vee and I talked about it. Just to air my doubts helped. She, after all, was one of the first people I had known to be associated with the antinuclear cause.

"You've got to remember," she would say gently, "we are in some ways fortunate. There are always dangers for our children. But had we been born a thousand years ago it might have been worse. Then our dangers would have been marauding villagers from the next county raping the women and sticking the children's heads on spikes. It's never easy."

She was right. I remembered a favorite Celtic saying of my mother's: "The fate of the mothers of young children is that they are never without fear."

Vee was having her own difficulties. She was finding her married status increasingly taxing, even on her unflagging energy. Tony, a shopkeeper's son from the North who had made good on the strength of his own brilliance, was not content with a simple life. He still wanted to entertain lavishly, live in opulence, and have his wife play the grand hostess at elaborate dinner parties. They had Ford Thunderbird cars and Tony kept a pedigree whippet and a Yorkshire terrier almost as decorations.

I think Vanessa felt she too was part of his collection of rare objects and beautiful people. It was frustrating. Already, for her, the choices in lifestyles were becoming polarized by the youth movement, the eruption of new ideas in politics, music, fashion, and the arts that she and I could both feel surging around us.

She had not yet cast in her lot with the "revolution"; Antonioni had not yet approached her with the starring role in *Blow-Up*, one of the first pictures to capture on film the swinging London of the sixties. But she did watch, read, listen and learn. And I knew from our conversations after Corin and I came back from the States, when we would discuss the effect of Kennedy's politics and his death, the Presidency of Lyndon Johnson, the policies of our own Tory and Labor governments, that Vee would really much rather have a bunch of pirates and outlaws around her dinner table engaged in passionate conversation about changing the world than she would the staid, the famous and the rich guests whom Tony chose to entertain.

Vee had always empathized with the underdog. Now she knew there was a cultural change going on around her, and her natural alignment was with the radical Left.

For people just beginning, as Timothy Leary (later dubbed the high priest of acid) was saying, "turn on, tune in, drop out," the restrictions of old prejudices were beginning to seem like straitjackets. Truisms we had been told by our parents and teachers about class and color and creed, old mores handed down from our Victorian grandparents, no longer seemed so absolute. The idea of changing the world by "freaking out" and "making love, not war," was quite simply more exciting.

Vee was intrigued. She sensed the times were changing but wasn't quite sure how. We gave her an entree to the "alternative." We took her to places she could never have found by herself. She thought Corin and I, in touch with another culture, were rather trendy in a way that she wasn't. Sometimes we'd take her to nightclubs like Sybilla's, which was owned by Sir William Piggot Browne and Sybilla Edmonstone, both well-heeled aristocratic dropouts, part of a new social scene that encompassed rock stars and artists as well as members of the upper classes who were trying to shrug off their background. Vee was still the feted lady of Stratford, Mrs. Tony Richardson, the left-wing bluestocking. We were more streetwise. Our friends weren't stars, but they were involved with what was to become a youth revolution, which would in turn breed its own stars, people who would spearhead the changes that became the hallmark of the sixties.

Corin's Cambridge friends, people like Peter Cook and David Frost, had an irreverent style of satire popular not only in the theater and cabaret, but also on television. There was an interesting group of Oxford and Cambridge graduates who were beginning to change the face of entertainment. After the wild success of the hilarious review *Beyond the Fringe*, Peter Cook and Dudley Moore started a nightclub called The Establishment. At the same time *Private Eye*, a magazine drawn from the same vein of semipolitical satire and put together by equally irreverent Oxford graduates, was launched on the world—much to the horror of the real establishment.

The Establishment club became the center for people dedicated to achieving change through ridiculing the system—a place where any kind of outrageous statement could be made under the guise of entertainment. It became notorious as the only place in London to give Lenny Bruce a platform.

We took Vanessa there, and we took her to dinner at a club called The Pickwick, frequented by what was beginning to be known as the "alternative society." The night we went we were sitting next to Anita Pallenberg and Brian Jones of the Rolling Stones who, dressed identically, with their long blond fringes, enormous eyes and wide cheekbones, seemed to me like decadent twin angels. Already Brian was wearing eye makeup and his hair was as long as Anita's. Vanessa was much more riveted by them than they by her. She has never been in the least concerned to be "cool" and appears to pay less and less attention to what people think of her the older she gets.

This bizarre group of people had not yet infiltrated Tony and Vanessa's lives. But Tony was fascinated. Freaks always appealed to him. When he and Vanessa asked us to a party, Tony would say, "Do bring some of your friends," as though we were a race apart. He has always been obsessed by trends, style and fashion. Even in his movies he will introduce haphazardly into a scene, sitting at a table, drinking at a bar, a stylish someone with a "name" to lend an avant-garde flavor.

Tony, a good ten years older than Vee, always liked to feel he knew what was happening on the "scene." He made it his business to be able to walk into any room and instantly identify whoever was there. He instinctively knew who had his finger on the pulse of change or who could define the nuances of fashion. He sought out those who were catalysts and symbols. He was in his element in London in the sixties, when that city was so obviously the flamboyant center of an emerging new world.

Vee was like a fish out of water. She looked slightly askance at whatever was going on, as though she couldn't quite understand why people dressed as they did, behaved so freely, broke so many rules. She had a detached air, rather like Michael, as though however scintillating the company or mesmerizing the activity, she would never be a part of it. She would watch, intrigued, but not be involved. Observe, but not experience.

As Tony would bend, sway or double over with the current trend, depending on how enthusiastically he viewed it, Vanessa would remain upright and entirely herself. She told me that she felt vulnerable and unsure much of that time, but she appeared invulnerable. Corin was much the same way. He was not able to relax and enjoy new ideas or styles the way Tony and I were. He stood quietly to one side and watched, only joining in if I absolutely insisted.

As different as we were, Vanessa and I were getting to know and like each other, connected by the common bond of pregnancy. Through our friendship, I began to feel that as much as I could learn from her about babies, the theater, and how a woman *could* encompass both motherhood and a career, I could also share with her my ability to simply enjoy myself, to cull from the changing times ideas that enhanced our day-to-day living.

It was a wonderful time for me. At last I was cracking my husband's elusive family—I was gaining the trust of the person who was perhaps the closest in the world to Corin. And I was having his baby. I woke in the morning with a feeling of joy, my life tingling with anticipation. I walked and walked in the fresh outdoors as the blaze of autumn burned itself out and winter chilled the streets and parks. I took pleasure in striding through the city, knowing that when I returned home to Corin a fire would be crackling and I would have preparations to make for our baby.

Sometimes I walked to Chiswick, where I visited Vanessa. As we grew enormous together, we shared the secrets of pregnancy, and the discomforts were lessened by knowing someone else was experiencing them too, by knowing we could talk about them, laugh and find a solution. Vee had cures for swollen ankles, aches and pains, indigestion, sleepless nights and even the sudden cold moments of apprehension that assailed me in the middle of the night. At those times it struck me with frightening certainty that what I was doing was incurring a responsibility that would change the whole of the rest of my life.

"One of the ways to deal with *that*," Vanessa said, looking at me knowingly, "is to be nice to yourself. Having a baby *is* hard work, and you're right, it always will be. Doesn't do to fool yourself, but it does help to treat yourself. Let's have a delicious lunch."

We both loved Italian food, and pregnancy certainly didn't blunt my appetite for herbs and spices and the rich textures of her Mediterranean cooking. We ate like horses, drank the best wine from her cellar. Then she would insist that we lie down with our feet higher than our heads (more restful), and by the time I got home to Corin I was feeling marvelous again.

One day when I was feeling particularly low and lumpy, she urged me to go shopping for something frivolous that would give me a lift and make me feel beautiful instead of frumpy.

So I trudged out into the foul weather of late December, searching for something, anything, that could transform me. But everywhere I looked were impossibly skinny girls in impossibly short skirts, and beside them I felt like a dowdy dowager. The generous curves of pregnancy made the day's styles out of the question for me, and I despaired.

The snow drifted down on the bustling King's Road. I went home, weeping a trail of tears into the slush.

Corin was wonderful. When I dragged myself home that day he took one look at my woebegone face, gave me a bear hug and, as he did on other days, made me a steaming cup of tea. He took off my shoes, rubbed my back, gave me a hot-water bottle and tucked me into bed.

"You're wonderful," he said, smiling at me with true tenderness. "You're beautiful. You're much more beautiful than you were before you were pregnant. I love feeling my baby move in your stomach. You're the most beautiful woman in the world to me."

I knew I was terribly lucky. Corin was helping me to love my body through its enormous change. I realized not all men would. His support helped me go through that difficult transition when a woman changes from sex object to mother, and sometimes feels she will stay sexless forever.

My daughter was born on the night of January 14, 1965, in the middle of a tempest.

I started in mild labor at about ten in the morning. Once I realized that the odd twinges of pain in my lower abdomen were actually my baby announcing its imminent arrival in the world, Corin and I drove to the hospital together.

I changed into my nightdress and was put in what was called "the waiting room."

The nurses brought me cups of tea and chatted brightly. Corin stayed as long as he could to make sure I was settled and was told that I probably wouldn't go into labor for hours. He decided he would have to go to his matinee. It was only as the nurse was taking my own nightdress and tying me into a white sterilized gown that I suddenly looked up at Corin putting on his coat, wearing the distant "goodbye" look that usually came over him when he had made up his mind to leave. It never failed to shock me how completely and suddenly he could cut off. If it was time to go, he went. If he no longer wanted to deal with a situation, he left it behind.

At that moment I knew precisely and completely the isolation of woman. I knew that I, and only I, could bring forth life from my body; only through me could this little baby inside me breathe, walk, talk. I was alone. I was afraid. For a moment I was paralyzed by loneliness, frozen by resentment at my fate.

By about nine that evening the pain had become intense. The nurse handed me a small plastic cup full of pills.

"Take these, my dear," she said. "Give you a good night's sleep."

"But I don't want drugs, and I don't want a good night's sleep," I said indignantly. "I told the sister when I came in that I wanted to have the baby naturally if I could. And I'm in labor now, so how can I go to sleep?"

I was already using my breathing exercises as I felt the waves of contractions more and more frequently. It was difficult to argue with her as well, but eventually I convinced her that I was indeed "on my way," as she put it. As she said it was only the beginning and that it would be hours before anything serious happened, I must take the pills and get some sleep to build up my strength. She predicted that I would not deliver until the morning.

I took the pills.

An hour later I felt the first really strong contraction. The pain shocked me out of a deep, drugged sleep. So *this* was what it was going to be like. Fear brought sweat shooting to the surface of my skin, and I tried desperately to convince myself to breathe slowly, to relax, not to fight the pain.

At about midnight Corin came back to the hospital, having finished his night performance. I was already well into mine. Trying to muster some semblance of dignity, struggling to remember the intricate breathing pattern I had learned. I felt embarrassed. Even in that agony I felt apologetic, as though I was causing too much trouble.

"Don't worry about rubbing my back, darling," I said. "How

was the theater tonight?" A screech of pain would tear the words out of my mouth. Corin's anxious face hovered over me as he mouthed the breathing exercises and tried to help me deal with what was happening.

Surfacing again, I asked him silly things like "Have you eaten yet? Are you tired? It must be terribly late. Get the nurse to make you a cup of coffee."

It terrified me to be so out of control. I had been brought up not to give in to feelings, and now was nearly overwhelmed. I didn't want anyone to see my struggle, to know I was crying and that I couldn't cope. But of course I did cope. The miracle is that you do.

When I was wheeled back into my room, Corin was there, looking as dazed as I felt. I took in Rachel's bright bowl of flowers and heard again the wind howling at the windows. It felt as though we were in Wuthering Heights, or a ship at sea. I'd never known a storm like it in London, nor weathered an internal one before.

"You've just come through with flying colors," said my husband, as though I had won an Olympics gold medal. And Corin held my hand as they brought in our daughter. I've never seen him so overwhelmed before or since. At once shy and proud, nervous and confident, he seemed to jump from boy to man in front of my eyes, all due to this fragile little creature he held bundled in his arms.

My pregnancy had been spent in a state of expectation. Suddenly, within seconds, it seemed, we were a family. Corin and I smiled at each other.

Elation colored the whole of the next day. I received flowers and telegrams and visitors, and Corin spent all the time with us that he could when he was not on stage. Our peaches-and-cream baby we called Jemima. Slowly and carefully I learned how to hold her, cuddle her, put her to my breast.

But by the second day, a wash of depression swept over me. I felt terrible. My breasts were hard as rocks before the milk came through properly, and every bone in my body ached with exhaustion.

As if to spite my girlish dreams, motherhood did not come as easily as all the books and discussions had suggested.

Once I returned home I found I would lie awake at night, nerves stretched to the point where sleep was impossible, waiting for the moment my baby would wake up demanding more of me. Even though she might be quiet, she could wake at any time. So I'd stay alert, forcing my eyes open. Hour after hour, I listened to her quiet murmured breaths, waiting for the restless stirring, the little cry, the signal that she needed me.

When Jemma did wake, I fed her. I held her in my arms, placing her mouth on my nipple and feeling her pliant, sweet-smelling warmth. The best times were when Corin would wake too, bring me tea and talk to me while I was feeding her, and his goodness and love made me feel better about everything. I couldn't tell him about my ghostly doubts and vexations; in the bright electric light of 6 A.M. they evaporated.

By the time the ritual was over, Jemma asleep again, nourished by me, burped by Corin, quiet, and I was slipping half-conscious into the womb of our bed, I would feel only that it was my fault—all the doubts, the anger, the fear—that it was only my nature that was complicating everything. If there was something missing, then it was missing from me. My fears had no right to be voiced, to be heard. I loved my husband. I loved my baby.

As the cold winter months passed and spring blossomed into life, so did I. I adjusted to motherhood, and the doubts melted with the snows. Both Corin and I were determined that Jemma would not lead a confined nursery life, so she came everywhere with us. I had decided against a rigid regime. She fed when she wanted, slept when she wanted and was cuddled when she wanted. It seemed to work.

Through it all, I was aware of a new sense of relief, a justification for my life. Now I had a reason for being in the home; for not wasting my time on a boring job; for getting up in the morning and going to sleep at night.

A pattern that pleased me was emerging. I was nurturing, so I was worthy of love. I had not realized just how useless marrying into a family of superachievers had made me feel.

12

Close Relations

During the months of my pregnancy and the weeks after Jemma's birth, I spent a great deal of time with Michael. We shared a passion for playing cards, and often in the evenings I would put Jemma in her carrycot, drive round to the Knightsbridge flat, and play kaluki or canasta with my father-in-law while my daughter slept peacefully.

We would play while Corin was at the theater. Michael, his friend and our best man Fred Sadoff, and various other friends would happily while away the hours gambling with small amounts of money and large amounts of enthusiasm. I would feed Jemma between games and then return to our own flat in time to cook dinner for Corin.

Rachel was never there for these gatherings, and I began to find it odd how little time she and Michael spent together. It was apparent they had a completely different circle of friends. Even if the whole family spent an evening together, Michael would inevitably rise at the end of the evening and announce that he was going out. He was always mysterious about where exactly he was going.

It was becoming clearer and clearer that the fabric of Redgrave family life was not quite as tightly woven as I had thought when we first met; and that Michael was aloof from the mainstream of family life. More often than not, he was also absent from gatherings at the country home.

"He prefers a cosmopolitan life," was the way family members explained it, making it sound as though he felt Odiham were a suburban cage.

In the atmosphere of obvious family tensions, Lynn and I grew closer. It was now about a year after Jemma's birth, and I decided I should get my figure back properly. Lynn was feeling the same thing about the weight she had had to put on to star in *Georgy Girl*. To go on working in films, which she now wanted to do, she knew she had to take it off. And quickly.

"I can't bear to look in a mirror any more," she wailed. "Having seen my horrible, ugly bulk on the huge screen, I have got to do something about it. I hate diets that last for ages. Let's go to a health farm."

"I don't know if I am self-disciplined enough to bear the regime," I replied. "Don't they give you any food at all?"

"Nothing," said Lynn, who had been before, "but you get used to it. Come on, Dee, it will be fun if we go together. We can have a laugh, there are always such strange people there."

I dubiously agreed. But it was going to be difficult to find someone to stay with Jemma, and it was the first time I had left her during that whole first year of her life.

Rachel and I had also become very close. She adored the baby and was continually asking us all down to Odiham so she could spend time with her granddaughter. I thought I could ask Rachel to have her to stay for a few days. She knew I was worried by a waistline that had still not returned to normal, and would approve of the fact that I wanted to pull myself together physically.

When Rachel agreed to the plan unhesitatingly, it made me think how silly I was not to ask for help more often. This was my family, too. My own mother was far away in the Mediterranean and I could no longer count on her support.

With a sigh of relief I thanked Rachel, telephoned Lynn to say it was all arranged, and a week later the two of us set off in Lynn's car. We were both very hungry because Lynn had persuaded me not to eat anything the day before leaving in order to get the most benefit from our fast.

"Alan Bates told me how one time he went to a health farm to lose weight for a film, and on the way down he got into such a panic that he ate a whole jar of crystallized fruits, and it took him the entire week just to get back to normal," she explained.

I felt like stopping and buying a jar of anything, but Lynn was very strong-minded, so I didn't want to let my side down.

Lynn had had trouble with her weight for some time. Like many teenage girls she had a habit of either binging or starving, something which I had done myself before I met Corin, and understood very well.

The pains and insecurities of adolescence were made much more complex for Lynn because she was emerging as a young woman in the shadow of her thin, beautiful older sister, already a star. Lynn always felt second best. Vanessa had even been offered the role in *Georgy Girl* by director Silvio Narizzano before Lynn. But despite being second choice, Lynn turned the part around quite brilliantly and made it fiercely her own, winning awards and praise and putting herself firmly on the same platform as her sister. Corin, although enjoying some success in the theater, was certainly in third place in the star stakes, although it never seemed to worry him much.

Corin simply did not see himself primarily as an actor. He seemed not to need to compete for theatrical laurels because the realm in which he reigned was the intellect. First and foremost, he was a scholar, a man of exalted intellectual power. He had already proved his worth by the age of twenty when he had gained his double first. It was like receiving an Oscar would have been for the rest of the family and he never felt jealous of his sisters' or father's accolades.

None of the outward trappings of success seemed to tantalize him. Not a vain man, he did not care to be photographed, did not want to be pushed by agents or pulled by promoters. He was only mildly amused when, as his career progressed, he began to receive fan mail. He always remained reluctant to sign autographs or talk to people who recognized him in the street.

It did not worry me that he had such an offhand attitude to the symbols of success. In fact, I admired the way he remained so untouched by flattery. We often met ridiculously vain actors, and I was proud of Corin's integrity. I knew how unusual it was in the entertainment business, where narcissism flourishes, to find such rigid adherence to a personal code of values.

But I did lend him my advice on style. He paid absolutely no attention to his appearance when I first knew him, unless, of course, he was on stage. By the time we had been together for a year or two, he was at least aware of how he looked, and even if he thought it foppish to care about clothes, he enlisted my help.

So I started buying his wardrobe for him, chose where he had his hair cut, and I even turned in his square-framed horn-rimmed spectacles for a pair which made him look much less like an old professor.

Lynn thoroughly approved of the slow transformation. She loved her brother and had always teased him for being a bookworm. She was happy to see him coming out of himself a bit more, loosening up, relaxing and laughing.

Lynn and I had been good friends from the day I first met her at Odiham. We shared an irreverent sense of humor, although her brilliance at mimicry and wit as a raconteur put her well out of my league and often reduced me to helpless laughter.

I knew that going to a fat farm with this sister-in-law would be a good time if it was nothing else. We set off on our mission impossible with a feeling of glee and complicity, like naughty schoolgirls. When I discovered a box of biscuits Lynn had hidden under the driving seat, I jogged her elbow so hard she nearly drove off the road.

Needless to say, we arrived with rumbling stomachs. Grayshott Hall was a rambling old Gothic mansion, with dozens of bedrooms, built of granite and set in the rolling lawns so typical of England's great houses. This one indeed had belonged to a rich landowner, who had later to sell his property as the cost of keeping up such grandeur accelerated.

We checked in and were shown to our comfortable double room, complete with wall-to-wall carpet, French windows and color TV.

"I hope this is not about to be the end of a beautiful friendship," I said dubiously. "Two starving people sharing a room are liable to get extremely ratty and irritable. Perhaps we won't be on speaking terms in a few days."

Lynn threw her Scrabble board on her bed. "As long as you don't cheat at this all the time, we might survive," she said.

We started our glorious regime. Glass of hot water with slice of lemon for breakfast. Same for lunch, same for tea, same for dinner. It was always produced with ceremony as if it were caviar.

"I don't know why they bother," I said to Lynn as we were sitting in the dining room. She was sucking on the slice of lemon as if it were a hamburger. "We could bring our own lemons and get the water out of the tap."

"It wouldn't be the same, Dee. If you make the effort to stagger along to the dining room and sit at a table, psychologically you think you have had a meal."

"Well I don't feel as if I have had one, it isn't working in my case, I can't stand this much more," I said miserably.

At this point a large, desperate-looking man in a dressing gown came up and addressed us. We had noticed him muttering to himself in the corridor.

"I have been arguing with my stomach for the last three hours," he moaned. "My stomach has won and I'm off to the local restaurant. Would you like to come with me?"

I was about to leap to my feet when Lynn confronted him furiously. "Begone, Foul Tempter," she said. "Snake within the castle walls, begone!"

So my hero shuffled off alone in the direction of the car park and I was left to wrestle with the demonic pangs of hunger.

Lynn and I were massaged and pummeled mercilessly; we sat in boiling steam baths, sweated our hearts out in saunas, exercised as if we were training for the Olympics and must have set up a record for lengths in the swimming pool.

The weight began to drop off, and hitherto forgotten bones began to emerge and hollows under the cheeks to appear. I began to enjoy it.

One person I knew there was Vidal Sassoon, who was with songwriter Hal Shaper. He came to the health farm at least twice a year and was an expert on nutrition and the healthy way of life. He would eye my endless cigarette smoking with suspicion and look with horror at my invariably uncoiffured hair; he nicknamed me "split ends," an accurate observation. But the Grayshott regime must have caused some improvement in my overall appearance. Late one evening he suggested that he and I should go for a swim in the large heated pool. We were alone. I dived in and, trying my best to look like Esther Williams, swam gracefully to the far end and waited for Vidal. He dived in and swam toward me underwater. Suddenly a complete stranger popped up in front of me. I was panic-struck and swam back looking desperately for Vidal, who I assumed must have drowned. "Have you seen my friend?" I called to the stranger. "But we are alone here, Deirdre," replied an astonished Vidal. His hair, which he usually wore Beatle style, like a helmet glued to just above the eyebrows and over the ears, had been swept back by the water, and uncharted wastes of never before seen forehead and ears had emerged, completely changing his appearance. I gaped at him in astonishment. I think he thought I was a mad person. Our evening's rendezvous ended with him fleeing for the changing room and me, convulsed by giggles, stumbling back to tell Lynn.

The week finished with Lynn and me returning to London feeling cleansed, slim and beautiful, suffused by a feeling of smug superiority induced by having mortified the flesh.

Later that summer, as I was eager to show off my now slim

body on the beaches of my youth, Corin dragged me onto a plane and we departed once more for a holiday in Malta. It was short-lived. After two days, his agent called with an offer to start shooting immediately in the film *A Man for All Seasons*. It was his first big film part, playing Susannah York's husband. He could not turn it down and returned immediately to London. Lynn, still slender, arrived at my parents' home to take his place for the planned holiday.

Malta with its colonial lifestyle was a complete change for us both. Lynn worked hard at her career, and in many ways so did I, at home with a demanding husband and child. We did not have anyone to assist us. But in my parents' home, things were very different. My mother and father had a chauffeur, a live-in cook, a housekeeper, a live-in cleaning lady and several dailies to oil the wheels of their life. All the domestics adored children and took Jemma over completely. She was treated like a little prin-cess. So without my daily commitment as mother, without Lynn's and my normal responsibilities to household chores, we were free to live the life of irresponsible adolescents. Breakfast in bed. Chauffeured to the beach in the morning. Chauffeured back again at lunch time. Siesta, and then our pick of eligible bachelors to escort us to the island hot spots. And escort us they did. It was like being out of school for the holidays. There were constant invitations to cocktail parties and dinner parties, fol-lowed by dancing beneath the palm trees under a starlit sky. Returning home, it was coffee and girls' chat, and Lynn telling me how much she loved acting for the independence it gave her, how she missed horses, but not riding in competition, and that at that point in her life she really had no desire for marriage or any emotional commitment beyond the theater.

"I never knew Malta would be such fun," Lynn said, sipping her coffee and liqueur. "Everyone is so friendly, and your family is so sweet to me. I'm having a wonderful time."

"Well, Lynn," I said honestly, "your family has always given me such hospitality it makes me happy to be able to do the same for you. Without you and Rachel, Vanessa and Tony and Odiham, I would miss my own family terribly and there would be a great lack in my life."

"I bet it wasn't so easy to begin with," said Lynn astutely. "I can't imagine what it must be like marrying into our madness. It's as though you automatically inherited a past that wasn't your own."

"What's that Shakespeare said? 'What's in a name?'—Well, we all know damn well there's a lot to a name, especially if it's well known!" I laughed.

"Well, I think you've handled it terribly well," she said comfortingly. "I don't really know if Corin takes his nose out of his books long enough to realize the sort of changes you've had to cope with, but he should be proud of you. You're still very much you, but you're at ease in any Redgrave-oriented situation without making a big deal out of it."

She also told me how much more relaxed and open and humorous she found Corin since he had been married to me.

She had had time by then to see the differences between my own family, with its rigidly conformist background of colonialism, and hers. My parents' favorite topics of conversation still revolved around schools and games and possibly local government—certainly not world politics or the latest art exhibition or artist to take the media by storm. My father still read only *The Times*. Reunions with his rugger-playing friends seemed to be the main source of social excitement for my dad, and Mum was still wearing the same floral-patterned silk dresses to the same kind of cocktail parties with the same nice, rather traditional people, as she always had.

But their way of life was very safe in its predictability. I loved my parents deeply, however rebellious I might have been in the past, and Lynn could see and feel the warmth between us all. I think she felt secure in its unspoken unchanging stability. Day was day and night was night in this family. It would probably have driven Lynn crazy had she stayed for longer than a fortnight. But for that length of time the two of us basked in the sun and luxuriated in the cushioned comfort of my parents' generosity.

I was pleased to be able to offer her this restful time. These were contented days that helped consolidate a real friendship with Lynn.

My sister-in-law flew back to London tanned and healthy to start work on another film. I was stuck with my old fear of flying. Airplanes to me were still like deadly monsters, and the air the most threatening place in the world to be. I told my parents I would return by train through Italy.

It was then that I began to feel peculiar. My body was not obeying its normal patterns. Briefly I wondered whether traveling had thrown off my balance, but after waiting a week for my period, I knew I was pregnant. The island had performed its secret fertility rite again.

I was quite horrified, and my mother, who thought a woman's role was to be wife and mother, couldn't understand my attitude. I felt confused and guilty.

Nauseous and moody, with Jemma still in nappies and my ankles beginning to swell, I set off in the prickly heat wave of an oppressive Mediterranean August to journey through Sicily, Italy and France to London. The journey was unspeakable. I noted that the attitude to children changed radically as we sped northward. On the Italian express, the guards and passengers were quite happy to play with Jemma, to my profound relief. In France, they were also quite friendly, but once I was on the Golden Arrow from Paris to Victoria Station all I heard was "Why can't you keep your bloody child under control?"

I was past keeping anything under control. The strain of the journey and the knowledge of my pregnancy had taken its toll, and I collapsed into Corin's arms the minute I saw his dear familiar face waiting on the platform.

"I'm going to have another baby, Cor," I said, handing him Jemma's damp little body as I got into the car to go home. "I feel awful."

But Corin was elated. "Another baby, Dee? My God, how

wonderful!" He was hugging me and Jemma at the same time and a grin split his face from ear to ear.

"But it's not wonderful," I whined morosely. "I'm really upset. I don't want to be pregnant again. Once is enough."

"But you can't have just one baby, Dee. What are you talking about? We want lots of babies. . . ." I had never considered this thought and looked at my husband as if he was a total stranger. *He* wanted lots of babies. I wasn't sure how I felt about even two!

I retired to my room in a state of utter depression. I did not completely reject the idea of having another baby, but I felt it was too soon to face the thought of another nine months of being sick and fat, another year of sleeplessness and another two of spending just about twenty-four hours a day scrambling after a heap of energy that seemed to do little but drain my own.

One of my greatest fears was that Corin would be out of work again and we would not have enough money to stretch for the needs of two children. I was being neurotic, of course. Corin was now appearing in *Lady Windermere's Fan*, a successful revival which also starred Coral Browne and Juliet Mills—daughter of John, sister of Hayley—who lived opposite us. Juliet and I became great friends. She and Corin had much in common. They both had famous acting fathers, and sisters who were more successful than they were.

Juliet was a very pretty woman in that pale-skinned, fair-haired, blue-eyed English way. She was having serious marital problems, which she confided to me. Her American husband, Russell Alquist, had hit the hippie culture hard and had absorbed the dropout mentality, one foreign to Juliet, who was struggling to look after her son and achieve success in the commercial theater.

She was the first friend I had who was actually supporting her child and trying to be independent, although in fact she had never sought it. She had enjoyed her marriage, loved her husband, and was miserable when he turned away from her and his family to look for happiness in a new philosophy. It was something I would learn about years later.

Then I was preoccupied with the immediate and overwhelming problem of an unwanted pregnancy. I lay in bed and thought about the carefree days Lynn and I had spent in Malta, when I was just beginning to feel that I had rediscovered my body, a feeling of freedom stemming from obeying only my own schedule, regardless of the needs of any dependents.

I felt trapped, and childishly, I sulked. I did not come out of my room for days, except to take care of Jemma's needs. I gave in to nausea, exhaustion and depression. I did not wash my hair, have a bath, or clean the flat. I knew I was being impossible but just didn't seem able to do anything about it.

One morning I lay in bed, green-faced and complaining, watching Corin getting ready to go out. I was gearing up for a scene.

"Where are you going?" I grumbled, hoping I was making him feel guilty about leaving me with a crying child, feeling ill because I was bearing his offspring. "What about helping me with the washing up?" Piles of dishes were congealing in the sink.

"I have a rehearsal with Claire Bloom this morning for our recording of *As You Like It.*"

Claire Bloom—that did it! I have always considered her to be wickedly beautiful. Suddenly unbidden memories of my mother issuing dark warnings about "losing your man through letting yourself go" flew into my mind.

I felt a sudden pang of fear. What on earth was I doing lying in bed until lunchtime? My hands instinctively flew to my stomach, where I could feel the slight swell of my abdomen, and to my already thickening thighs. I sighed. The flat, tight firmness of a few months ago was gone again.

I jumped out of bed and peered into our rather dusty mirror. My hair looked awful, as though I'd at the very least been dragged through a haystack backward. I had no makeup on, my skin looked papery white, but there were no signs of ill health. Of course not—I wasn't ill. I was just pregnant, and insecure about being pregnant partly because I thought I would be unattractive to my attractive husband. I knew I would not have an abortion; it was strictly against my religious and humanitarian beliefs. And I knew I really did not want one. So I had to accept with grace the condition in which I found myself.

I looked through my jumbled wardrobe for fresh clothes, I took a bath and washed my hair and filled the flat with flowers. I did everything I could to make it the perfect home, so that when Corin returned I would be there, delicious smells emanating cosily from the kitchen. Me, the picture of the perfect wife.

He came home late in the afternoon and was amazed at the transformation of our flat, which when he left was reminiscent of a bomb site.

"What on earth happened?" asked Corin.

"Nothing," I said, acting as if it were all normal. "Can I pour you a drink?"

Corin was dumbfounded. I busied around, pouring him a drink, poking the fire, looking as glamorous as I could, as if nappies and nausea belonged to another race. But soon my curiosity took over.

"What was she like?"

"Who?" answered Corin.

Who? Who! Who indeed?

"Claire," I said, trying to sound casual.

"Very nice, a friendly woman," he replied offhandedly.

Well, "a friendly woman" certainly did not sound too threatening! I began to relax. I thought I should try to explain my boorish behavior of the last few weeks. I attempted to describe my fear, my resentment at getting "caught" again, and my dread at the thought of so many more years of responsibilities and bills when we still had so little money.

"But I'm working now," Corin reminded me. "I'm making money and I'll go on making money. I'll always take care of you and the kids. You know that."

Did I? I looked at him. I hoped so. Maybe even then I wasn't quite sure.

"You are my woman, my mate, my love," he said, and put his hand gently on my stomach. "I love you. You don't need to be so afraid."

I hugged him for reassurance. I reminded myself that there was no reason to doubt. At this point in our lives I had no reason to disbelieve him.

13

Betrayal

Late in 1966, Corin accepted a role in a television series opposite sexy Susan George, who was then stepping into Julie Christie's shoes as a cross between an English rose and a blond bombshell. The series, called "The Newcomers," took off. It was in the 6:30 P.M. evening slot, which catches the family viewers, and before long his face was being recognized in all the local shops, and his fan mail swelled. Corin played boyfriend to both Susan George and Judy Geeson, another up-and-coming English actress in the same curvy blond mold. For the first time he began to be considered something of a ladies' man. People looked at him in a slightly different way. He had a sexier air about him than the cool professor I married had ever had, and for a while we both enjoyed his success as the attractive young hero figure of British television.

The BBC then asked him to play the lead in a new serial, "The Tenant of Wildfell Hall," from the book by Anne Brontë. This time he was to play a character based on Bramwell Brontë, an antihero—a caddish husband and good-looking reprobate.

Corin looked quite wonderful in the dashing clothes and swirling cloaks of the period, and gained an immediate and further following of female viewers.

That was the year that Corin Redgrave, without even trying, joined the lineup of handsome young British actors who were making Britain a leading force in the world of television, cinema and theater. He, Ian McShane, John Hurt, Edward Fox and Michael York epitomized the public's idea of England's blue-eyes boys and were also respected as accomplished actors who could lend some of their own wild ways to a part and stamp it with originality.

Success transformed the lives of Corin's contemporaries. Each one of them has made his mark, especially on cinema, and each one is now able to pick the choicest parts and command astronomical salaries.

Corin, however, remains an actor of immense power who has never quite clicked. He was offered, and to this day is still offered, good parts, but never the key role. I never understood why, and it never appeared to concern Corin. So the weeks rolled by, and we had just enough money, and Corin was just enough known for our lives to be gay, amusing and filled with stimulating people and exciting possibilities.

The fact that my husband's formidable will was not focused on advancing his career did not strike me then as peculiar. My role was still that of the accepting wife. I was putting my bit in more often now, giving him my opinion, discussing my ideas, but still it was his career, not mine. I believed, and at the bottom of my heart I knew, that he knew enough about the world to be able to juggle the possibilities and come up with the answer he wanted.

Our second child, our son Luke, was born on April 9, 1967. He was a sweet and gentle baby, unlike Jemma, now two, who had become a turbulent, difficult but utterly fascinating child.

While I was in hospital after having Luke, Lynn came to visit me. She had just flown back from New York, where she had not only received critical acclaim for her performance in *Black Com-*

edy, but had also found a husband, an expatriate English actor named John Clark. They arrived at my bedside carrying flowers and presents, Lynn glowing with her new-found happiness.

Marriage suited her. She was twenty-four and radiant. *Slim* and radiant. Her now assured recognition as an actress in her own right and her emotional stability served to end her need for "binging" as efficiently as marriage and motherhood had for me.

She told me how the whole family had welcomed John, delighted at her happiness. As the years passed, John proved himself to be a very forceful man. He gave new impetus to Lynn's career, becoming for a while her manager, then her producer and director. It was he who helped finally to persuade Lynn to go to live and work in America, where she had become the darling of television audiences, with her own weekly series "House Calls," in which she played a slightly eccentric hospital administrator to well-groomed perfection, and also became a focus for feminists with her battle against the TV network to allow her to breastfeed her child on the set. But she has succeeded in putting far more than an ocean between her and a family that has made quite different life choices.

But these were the days when we were all still close, and Lynn had not yet lost her British accent.

I was delighted when she arrived. I knew I was going to be lonely. I had a new baby, and Corin was due to fly out to Turkey in a fortnight, to work for months on a new, big-budget British film he was starting: *The Charge of the Light Brigade*. Vanessa was in it too. They would have each other for company, but I was looking at a good four months on my own. I was more than relieved at that moment to know that the most accessible and friendly member of the family would be around in case of emergencies.

Corin was delighted, too. He was worried about me being alone with two small children and no help.

He wanted me to go with him. "Why don't you come out there, Dee?" he asked. "Tony [Richardson] is directing it. That will be fun, and it will be lovely for you to have a holiday." But I thought two children in nappies in that wild location would be an impossible strain on both of us, so I settled myself down for what I thought would be a quiet domestic spell for a few months on my own.

I had always found his departures unsettling—having to get used to making a life for myself when he was away on a movie, and then, adjusting again to his needs and demands, my change of role from independent woman back to actor's wife, when he returned.

His departure to work on the film meant that we were once again reasonably well off, and were able to move from Vanessa's flat into our own home. It was a lovely Victorian flat in a mansion block called Coleherne Court, with enough bedrooms for all of us and a room for an au pair girl. That was my greatest luxury— help with the children.

I had the time and space to start seeing friends I had not seen in a while, some of whom had transformed themselves into dope-smoking, acid-dropping mystics. I had removed myself from old friends for too long, but was determined to catch up on lost time.

I bought Indian bedspreads and converted them into the long dresses I saw other people wearing. I wore a bell on a leather thong around my neck and took my children to the "love-ins" held regularly in Hyde Park, wandering among the hippies sitting cross-legged on the grass, the smell of marijuana wafting across the crowd, rock and roll rippling through ancient trees as though to shake off their leaves in time with the shaking hips of long-haired dancing girls.

Everybody looked young, pretty, free from burdens and very stoned. I didn't feel totally at ease. Altering lifestyles was one thing, altered consciousness quite another.

I didn't ever take LSD, which put me outside a certain realm of experience and a tight circle of people who were drug experimenters. To me the sixties culture was never completely innovative. It seemed to be borrowed from so many things, from the mysticism of the East, the philosophies of a dozen different ages and civilizations, from the black-leather rebellion of the fifties, from music which had its roots in music I had been listening to for years, from a naive idea of social change and a coming utopia which I did not really believe in, and most of all from mind-expanding drugs.

I did not want to take drugs because I had just had two babies. My body had hurtled through enormous changes in just three years and was still frail. Neither my mind nor my body was ready for the chemical and psychological cataclysm of LSD.

My mystical friends convinced me to smoke hashish, cheaper and better for you, they said, than nicotine or alcohol, and I tended to agree. And I did love the music of the culture, even as it grew more and more specific about drugs and their effects, and musicians more and more daring in their use, and often abuse, of them.

My dear friend Trisha Locke opened a fashionable new model agency called English Boy. She had worked for a well-known magazine in Italy and then for The Who; her sister was a successful fashion designer, and Trisha had a brilliantly perceptive eye. She saw how the male and female stereotypes were changing. Thanks to trouser suits and Vidal Sassoon's chopped hair, girls were looking like men. They were also behaving like men, getting jobs, riding motorbikes, demanding equality.

At the same time men were growing their hair below their shoulders, pushing their babies along the streets and wearing decidedly effeminate clothes. I attended the huge concert in Hyde Park where Mick Jagger wore a dress and was photographed by just about every newspaper in the world.

Trisha realized that men had crossed over to an overt recognition of the female elements of their nature and were showing it by the clothes they wore. The social changes taking place were being expressed and reflected through fashion, and for some reason this facet of the change seemed more marked in men than women.

So Trisha started English Boy as a model agency that would provide unconventionally striking men to be photographed, men who looked like desirable rock stars or handsome hippies. Instead of muscle-bound heroes with short haircuts and toothpaste smiles she offered models who were in keeping with the trends of the time.

Corin did not like this scene much. He had always been too serious to take more than a passing glimpse at what might be fashionable. When he was at home we lived a very private life with our children, which is why I so seldom saw my old friends.

When he went away to Turkey, my doors were opened again. I would find myself slipping down the King's Road to have coffee with Trisha in the little old house she called her office. There I would find myself in the middle of this bizarre parade where people wearing extraordinary clothes culled from junk shops and markets, expensive tailors and their grandmothers' wardrobes, would float in and out on wafts of patchouli oil and marijuana smoke. Sometimes it was hard to tell which was boy, which was girl.

Over the next few months, I discovered a world in which people my age and younger were living out what they called an "alternative culture." It meant sharing lovers, an abundance of sex, living in communes, trying out new diets, using herbal medicines, having babies without husbands, having jobs with husbands, having husbands without jobs. It was topsy-turvy, and far removed from my life as a Redgrave, which until then had seemed enviable and glamorous. All of a sudden I had to look again at what I was doing with my life.

I was not sure if I liked what I saw. It was clear that life as a member of the Redgrave clan was bypassing this present stage in the cultural explosion. Having prided myself on a sense of style and ability to carry off just about anything I wanted to, I found myself out of step, out of fashion, out of time. I looked at my friends and they were wearing twenties silks, Victorian petticoats, men's hacking jackets, American Indian turquoise, Eastern jewelry of every kind including ankle bracelets.

I would stagger back home to my kitchen, feeding my babies, changing their nappies, bound by their bedtimes and their mealtimes and their potty times until I felt like an automaton, bewilderingly isolated from what was going on around me. And in comparison to the peacock men and women of my age, dowdy again. Sometimes I wouldn't even go out of the house. I was still too "unenlightened" and too insecure to think I could be part of this new society unless I was linked to a man who was part of it.

So I missed Corin terribly, felt lonely and bored without him, was drawn back to the busy hubbub of "swinging London" whenever they took the trouble to persuade me I was really wanted.

Trisha knew I was fascinated by what was going on but shy of my role in it, and she made a special effort to include me. I remember going to one of her parties in Chelsea brimming over with people as bright as butterfly wings, and—or so it seemed to me from my place on the stairs where I was sitting feeling lumpishly maternal—quite as graceful.

These rare butterflies insisted on including me, talking to me, offering me joints, sweeping me up to dance and dance and dance.

Ah, now I knew what it was. They were having a *good time*. They wanted everyone to have a *good time*, to look good, to feel good, to do whatever made them feel happy. It all seemed quite simple suddenly. And the feeling of well-being was infectious. I felt good, too, for the first time in a long time.

I thanked Trisha and walked home dreamily through a dawn which could have been the dawn of the universe for me. I felt vibrant, lucky to be alive, roseate from unaccustomed attention. When I let myself into our flat I was thinking lovingly of my absent Corin and of my babies. I bent over the children's beds and kissed their softly breathing, sleeping faces.

"Tomorrow's Sunday," I thought, smiling as I slipped under the covers and shut out the light. Sunday meant I could sleep for a while and try to snatch some rest before the children pulled me out of my reverie.

I did sleep later than usual, but all too soon Jemma was scrambling all over me and Luke was wailing to be fed. I gave Jemma breakfast and took Luke into bed with me to feed him. As he snuggled into the crook of my arm contentedly, I looked at the smooth furry down on the top of his head, and across at Jemma's naughty little face and wondered how I could have become so snarled up by my own sense of inadequacy. I wasn't doing too badly at all. I had two beautiful children, a clever husband, a real home.

I felt at peace with myself and with what I had to offer those I loved. My months apart from Corin had taught me that the Redgrave name did not have to either annihilate me or absorb me. I had emerged from my cocoon and found, once again, that life is so invigorating when one participates in the world outside one's own small frame of reference. I could and would start to enjoy my life as much as my friends appeared to be enjoying theirs.

There was so much to look forward to. I was terribly eager to share it with Corin.

I finished feeding Luke, and Jemma brought me in the Sunday papers. The slight, unfamiliar blur of a mild hangover was clouding my brain. I took a sip of coffee, and as my eyes began to focus, vast black headlines took shape, proclaiming an earthquake disaster in Turkey. One thousand dead in Istanbul. Corin. My heart turned over. Corin was in Istanbul. My husband was in the middle of an earthquake, and I had no idea how to find him.

I could do nothing but wait for someone to contact me. The waiting that day was one of the most excruciating experiences of my life.

Finally, hours later, a woman designated by the film company to call all the families reached me.

"Everyone in the cast is safe," she said, although I hadn't even had time to ask a question. "Corin couldn't ring you because almost all the lines are down and communication is virtually impossible. But he'll be home in two days and he's perfectly all right."

She could tell me nothing of what had happened, but I was so extraordinarily relieved, almost to the point of total collapse, that I knew I could wait for details until Corin came home.

Late the next night he arrived back from Turkey.

I didn't know what time to expect him. No one knew what flight the cast would be able to get out of Turkey. I sat up for hours waiting for him, wondering what had happened, wondering if he would be all right, thinking how long the four months he had been away now seemed. Eventually I fell asleep waiting.

He let himself in with his own key and tiptoed into the bedroom to wake me.

"Deirdre." He sat down on my side of the bed and put his arm gently on my shoulder. He didn't kiss me. I sat up and looked at him. His hair was longer, long and blond, streaked by the sun, and his skin tanned. He was thinner, too, and his eyes pierced out of that golden face, their blue heightened by the sun's coloring.

He looked like a stranger. He felt like a stranger. I didn't know what had happened to create that chasm between us. Time of course, distance, many things.

It was late to talk. We were both tired. I pulled him down toward me and hugged him quickly, then got up to make us coffee while he undressed and got into bed. I noticed again how thin he was, and how tanned his body.

"Was it terrifying?" I asked quietly. It took him a while to answer but once he started, he repeated what had happened over and over again, as though he wanted to exorcise his own memory of what he had seen, the face of death in the yawning of the earth as its mouth opened and, like a great whale, swallowed indiscriminately anything it found.

"I was lying in bed in my hotel room," he said. "The hotel was high up on the side of one of the hillsides of Istanbul. When the first tremor shook the walls, I was flung right out of bed and landed on the floor. I'd never been in an earthquake before. We didn't any of us know what we should do. I just scrambled into my clothes, the first things I could find, and tore into the corridor. The stairs were jammed with hysterical people running for the ground floor in various stages of undress as second and third tremors reduced the building to a jelly. It was like being in a ship, the entire building was rocking backward and forward."

He put his head in his hands as though by shutting his eyes he could shut out the pictures and blank out the screams.

"When the tremors eventually began to subside we all crammed into the bar to get drunk," he said, and grinned for the first time. "There wasn't anything else we could do. If we had gone to the beach, we could expect a tidal wave. If we tried to drive, where could we go? The roads were caving in and rock slides made some of them impassable. The only thing left was to get drunk. So we did, waiting to see whether there would be anything further."

In fact, the worst was over. The quake had reached number 8 on the Richter scale. More than a thousand deaths were reported, and although the figures were hard to corroborate, much of the beautiful city was in ruins. My husband was lucky to escape with his life.

As the days at home went by, Corin seemed to regain his usual calm. All the cast were called upon to pull themselves together for the end of the shoot, which was scheduled for location in the English countryside. So of course he did.

But there was still something strange about him. A withdrawn air that was unfamiliar. I could not put my finger on it. We had been like lovers when he left. We had gone out to dinner every night, he brought flowers home, he'd hold my hand in the street and lie with his arms around me every night. Now that intimacy was gone, and I felt chilled without knowing why, or what had happened.

We were having breakfast one morning, about two weeks after Corin's return, when the mail arrived with a typewritten letter to Corin stamped with an Istanbul postmark. Corin opened it casually, wandered out of the dining room with it in one hand and a cup of coffee in the other.

"What's that?" I asked.

"Oh, just a hotel bill," he muttered by way of explanation, and walked into his study and closed the door.

This wasn't unusual. Whenever he had writing to do, or scripts to read, he shut himself away. I didn't think any more of it until he had left for location work, and I was on my own.

I was straightening up the flat. When I got to the study, I noticed there was no hotel bill lying around. That was odd. Corin usually left his opened mail in careless heaps. My nerves tingled with premonition, and I started to feel sick. It came over me in waves. When you know someone's behavior patterns so intimately, a change as simple as that takes on appalling significance. I wondered what to do. Should I look for the letter from Istanbul? I had never been the kind of person so driven by jealousy as to go through pockets looking for evidence of infidelity, for clues to deceit. I had always thought that beneath me. Beneath us. Ours was not that kind of relationship. We did not need that kind of subterfuge. Our love was based in trust. Thank God.

But today was different. This morning felt cold. I felt cold. My heart was fleeing my body.

I kept thinking, "Be dignified. You'll be the loser either way. Don't pursue fear." But I couldn't stop myself. I didn't have to look far. The letter was on the top of a lot of papers in the first drawer I opened. Corin had no idea how well I knew his habits. I read the first few lines of the passionate love letter, and my marriage, my identity, my faith in everything I knew fell apart. The pain was physical as well as emotional. I had opened Pandora's box and now I was paying the price.

It was a sparkling day, drops of sunlight falling like water on the full deep summer green of the trees lining the London pavements. I tried to walk for a while to clear my head. But everything reminded me of Corin and me before this disaster. I remembered how we would run in the park with Jemma, or would sit under the great leafy branches of the trees at Odiham when we first met. The song of the birds made me hurt inside. My rage was bubbling up like a geyser with no outlet until I felt I would burst, so I ran inside and lay crying helplessly on our bed.

I desperately wanted to confide in someone. My mother was still in Malta; I couldn't go to her. Rachel would have been my first choice because she had become almost a surrogate mother, but I didn't want to destroy her illusions, or rather, I didn't want to risk the possibility that hearing about her son's infidelity might hurt her as much as it had me.

Or maybe she would take this news—which to me seemed so ominous—lightly, as though such things were intrinsic to every marriage. Rachel, very much a woman of the world, had weathered great ups and downs in her marriage to Michael. I had seen how she coped with their life together. It was clear that the gifted actor was not an easy man to live with. Yet somehow, Rachel always emerged calm, controlled and beautiful. She always seemed like a ship in full sail, never shipwrecked, as I felt now. Vanessa also had this sort of grand control of her emotions and of circumstance which I found daunting and enviable. It was as though they could always stand, if not victorious, at least elegant, under any conditions. I felt incapable of pulling off that kind of performance, and incapable of subjecting my marriage with Corin to their scrutiny.

So I stayed alone and brooding.

I suppose that the first major betrayal in anyone's life has an indelible effect. The amount of pain one experiences is equal to the amount of faith and energy one has invested. I hoped I was not sufficiently arrogant to assume that Corin would be forever faithful to me, or me to him, for that matter. But being faced with the hard, and for me, frightening, reality of unfaithfulness, I knew those ideas were being put to the test of my (theoretical) tolerance.

I was shaking. I took some tranquilizers that my doctor had prescribed to help me sleep. They helped, and I was grateful to be living in the twentieth century.

I managed after twenty attempts to contact Corin on location and hysterically blurted out my news. It almost seemed as though he had been waiting for it. He said he would come straight home. I wandered up and down the flat the whole day, waiting for his return from the set.

I remembered my mother's advice: "Men hate scenes," so I tried to keep my feelings under control.

When I finally heard his key turning in the door I froze.

A phrase in the letter came winging back to me, circling my brain. "Your fingers on the keys call to me," she had written. And I suddenly remembered how he had sat down at the piano at Michael's flat that first night we met and had sung into my eyes.

Now he was singing to her. Who was she? How could he betray me like that?

I opened the door of the bedroom before he could close the door to the flat, and he whirled around. There was a look of shock on his face, like someone caught red-handed at some devious deed. Under his arm was a bottle of wine. And he thrust it towards me as he moved away from the door.

"Please come and sit down with me, Dee," he said quickly. "Before you even start your accusations you must know that I love you. You are the only one, the only one. . . ."

His arms were around me by now, his hands stroking my hair. I shook with tears inside his arms and he tried to calm me, but I pulled away.

All his words were placating and full of love, but they weren't enough. My soul had been carved in two and nothing he could say would ever change that, ever heal that wound.

I told him it was the first great betrayal of my life, and although I did still love him and was prepared to put on a good show, there was a breach between us which would never be crossed.

But I believe he thought he would reach me again, would reassure me, would convince me that the other relationship had been so superficial it should have no effect on our life together. He tried very hard, and for all our sakes, I tried to keep up the pretense.

That night we were due to attend a party given by Anna Massey. Corin begged me to go with him. Anna was Jemma's godmother. She would wonder what was wrong if Corin went without me. Perhaps he thought the party atmosphere would provide a needed distraction. So, screaming inside, I quietly put on my makeup and slipped into my embroidered velvet dress and took my husband's arm as though there were nothing in the world to worry about.

On arrival we were instantly surrounded by friends from the theater. They were delighted to see Corin and hear of his exploits filming *The Charge of the Light Brigade,* and of course everyone wanted to know about the earthquake. I felt alienated, and I wanted to be alone to cry.

There was a young married couple at the party holding hands, not wishing to be separated for a moment. I observed them with jaundiced eye, wondering how long it would be before one or the other destroyed their peaceful happiness. I felt hysterical. Corin was talking calmly to friends, relating anecdotes, the witty and intelligent center of attention.

I fled. I jumped into a taxi. All I wanted was to cuddle my children and forget about men and their needs. But before long, I found myself waiting for Corin's return. I was adjusting my makeup, putting on my most alluring nightdress so that he would look at me, respond to me, so that I could speak to him, using sex, the only strength I knew, as a way to reach him. I was in pain, but I knew the pain would be worse if I really lost him, so I prepared to do battle.

He returned. He did not wish to discuss the letter. He only said that it was from an overwrought woman called Janan with whom he had had a brief affair during the three long months of our separation, but that in no way should it affect me.

Not affect me! It had destroyed the very fabric of my existence. But for the sake of my own dignity I let Corin go to sleep in preparation for his early morning call. When all was peaceful, I went to the farthest room in our apartment, put a pillow over my head and screamed my pain. I continued this pattern for weeks. Once again I had to deny my feelings because I could not speak of them to my husband.

I became obsessed by the affair. Every news article I read, every novel, seemed to highlight my predicament. No easy escape. I felt the archetypal female victim. I felt that against all odds, circumstances, temptations, my first allegiance had been to the family unit that Corin and I had created. He had been unfaithful to me only months after I had given birth to our son, and I could not come to terms with his affair. Corin thought that the intensity of our feelings for each other meant that such meaningless experiences could be easily overcome, part of the common experience of working through a marriage—but since he never wanted to discuss the issue after that first day, it only festered in my mind.

One day the unit was shooting at Corin's family cottage in Odiham. We went down to spend the day, although the action involved Vanessa, not Corin. I met all the friends he had made during his months in Turkey. I became paranoid. I felt everybody knew Corin had been unfaithful to me.

That afternoon, Corin smoothly introduced me to the cast and crew as his wife. I even made sure I looked my best for the occasion and that I moved forward blithely to shake hands with, or say "Hi" to, whoever it was I was meeting. But inside I was trembling. As a woman I felt humiliated to the point of annihilation. I knew that everyone there knew Corin had been involved with another woman. I kept imagining snide conversations behind raised hands or closed doors. I could no longer see myself as anything other than an object of ridicule.

I felt so betrayed that I could not look at Michael, Rachel or Vanessa. All of them were there. I got hold of a bottle of wine and went for a long walk in the countryside by myself.

In retrospect, I suppose it is ludicrous that one affair should have had the devastating effect it did. Intellectually I knew that other liaisons in a marriage where the two people are necessarily apart for much of the time can, and frequently do, happen without disastrous effects.

I suppose also that the degree of fear, rage and panic that one feels in a situation like that is affected by one's own most profound feelings of self-respect, self-knowledge and security. I had to face my own real insecurity, and it took me many years to recover from the shock of what I found.

In the weeks that followed, during which Corin continued to work on the film and I tried to piece together my crushed ego, we spent little time together. Friends persuaded me to go out more often without him, and Trisha's companionship was an entree into the circle of people who were just beginning to give me such pleasure before Corin's return.

I began going out for lunches and light conversation, to allow the briefest of flirtations, to recover a sense of myself. I needed other people to confirm my own worth as a woman.

In the meantime, Corin's lover, Janan, came to England. My first knowledge of this visit came through a letter Corin wrote me from the film set. I froze when I recognized my name written in his handwriting on the envelope, but his first words reassured me that it was a love letter, and a letter of apology.

Corin wrote that perhaps his very happiness in our marriage had given him a false sense of security, a feeling that our love was so closely knit that nothing could unravel it. But he had realized that he had been wrong. Not about his love, which was unshakable, but about our relationship—that love was not the whole story. There is needed also a sure means to express it, a confidence and a trust. He thought our relationship was as firm and sturdy as our love, but it turned out to have been delicately balanced, built up through trial and error, over a long period of years, like a building that collapses when one essential stone is removed. He felt an oaf to have tampered with this delicate thing that now lay in fragments—and that he was not sure-fingered enough to put it together again.

He wanted, he needed, my respect as much as he needed my

love, and asked me to believe that what he had done he had done blindly and foolishly, not underhandedly or treacherously.

I was moved, and I hoped that—although I knew everybody perceives actions and events in a different way, always—Corin and I could at last come together again.

But then I read on. He continued to say that he now had to do what he felt he had to do, which was to see *her*. He was going to stay with Vanessa. He wanted me to know because he didn't want to deceive me. He said that he had never intended to continue the relationship, nor did he now, but still he had promised that he would see her when she came to London. He was anxious to clear up the matter with her, feeling he could do nothing for himself and nothing for us otherwise. He begged me to trust him and promised not to be unfaithful to me. He vowed to make it clear to her that he must and wanted to live with me and for me only.

Trust him. Trust the faithless husband.

One day Ben Arris, an actor friend of Corin's, pointed her out to me when I visited the set. Up until now I had only been able to fantasize Corin's Jezebel. She had appeared in myriad apparitions—as a mermaid spirit with flowing hair, a damsel in distress with raven's-wing tresses, a curvaceous piece of Turkish delight to sugar the tongues of all who tasted, even a vulnerable blonde as sexy and sweet as Marilyn Monroe, all ready to ensnare the withdrawn intellectual.

But in reality she was short, squarish and dark-skinned. Her hair might have shone in the sunlight of Istanbul but in the drizzle of a glorious English spring it looked simply damp. Bedraggled damp. A tan that might have glowed in the warm sun now looked sallow, almost yellow. The curves were there, but the hips too broad. My hips were flat and bony, and my legs long and my eyes quite as dark and flashing as hers—hers flashed only distress and suspicion once she realized who I was.

I began to feel stronger. I went to the pub with the crew and downed a few pints of the local brew. Suddenly all the black and threatening shadows of my dreams faded as the sun lit the daffodils bright, bright lemon, and I could walk at my husband's side without dying of self-doubt.

Much later, at the end-of-shoot party, I went in on the arm of Corin, with all my rediscovered confidence, and when we saw that she was there, still hanging around, we departed together. The taste of such hollow victory was not exhilarating, as I might have thought. Just rather bitter and disgusting, as though someone had fed me meat which had been in a tin too long.

14

The Radicalizing of the Redgraves

Life began afresh. Once Janan went back to Turkey, and *The Charge of the Light Brigade* was completed, Corin and I returned to a semblance of our old days of domesticity in Kensington, both trying very hard to stitch up the seams of a marriage that had been cruelly wrenched apart.

I threw myself once more into the role of wife and mother, pushing fears for the future out of my mind. Corin started a new film called *The Magus*, based on John Fowles's remarkable book of mayhem and magic. Anthony Quinn, Candice Bergen and Michael Caine were starring in it, and the location this time was Greece.

Corin had been fitted for his uniform as a sadistic Nazi officer when he first returned from Turkey. By the time they started filming, our mutual unhappiness had taken its physical toll and the uniform hung from his thin shoulders as if from a scarecrow. When I finally saw the film the only thing I noticed was how his neck grew out of his shoulders two inches smaller than the collar. The strain of those months seemed to me to be written across the screen as though someone had used indelible ink.

We had built walls of silence around ourselves, and I thought

I could draw Corin out of his tight world of intellectual detachment by turning on the sounds of the new culture and dragging him to meet the butterflies and peacocks, hoping he might find some common bond.

Corin was beginning to believe the right wing establishment might be evil, worthy of destruction, and that perhaps it should be replaced by extreme socialism, what Marx called the dictatorship of the proletariat. The people I took him to meet wished for the nonviolent destruction of the existing system, which they too saw as corrupt, power-hungry and dangerously balanced in favor of materialism. But like me, they took a lighter tack than Corin, believing in changing the system by living outside it, or creating an atmosphere where its impositions were at least temporarily irrelevant.

So I introduced him to the people I had met through Trisha. One of my favorites was a delightful man named Mickey Lumley, whose profession as successful fashion designer was far removed from Corin's field of activity, but whose brain was quick and incisive, and whom I felt Corin would enjoy if they could get to know each other. I was right. They did get to like each other and all three of us became close friends.

But most of those people I had hoped Corin might relate to turned out to be more interested in blowing their minds with hallucinogenics than doing anything significant. Their "peace and love" philosophy was far too soft-centered and flimsy for Corin.

Although Corin, out of a purely intellectual curiosity, did try LSD once, we both instinctively turned toward a more practical form of revolution.

As the year progressed, we became more involved in radical politics. Corin and I helped to organize, and took part in, demonstrations against the growing American involvement in Vietnam. Because the Redgraves had always veered to the left, their stand on Vietnam was inevitably against the American invasion. Already Vanessa had been in contact with Jane Fonda, whose inimitable voice was raised in passionate protest. (In May 1968, when her daughter was born, Jane named her Vanessa after my sister-in-law because she so admired the fearless way Vanessa had taken a stand against nuclear warfare.) However, that was as radical as Vanessa was in those days.

It was becoming clearer and clearer that the politics of love were not enough. The alternative culture was becoming polarized. There were those who believed that awareness of those who ruled the world could be changed by putting acid in the water of the White House, as it was rumored Grace Slick and Abbie Hoffman tried to do, or the House of Commons, as friends of mine advocated. On the other side of the fence, there were those who believed that following Marx would change the world, or that the answer to the gun was the gun.

Corin and I often argued over philosophies in those days. We were both trying to find a way that would work, but we approached it differently according to our past, and our basic natures.

My inclination was toward the kind of political anarchy put forward by the people who edited and wrote for the underground magazines such as *International Times* and *Oz*. My friends Richard Neville and Mick Farren had been taken to court for expressing views the Establishment branded as "obscene." My shift to the left had been as much influenced by rock and roll as by any Marxist tract. As Jerry Rubin pointed out rather flippantly: "Most of the New Left were born out of Elvis's gyrating pelvis."

Corin, on the other hand, despised the underground movement, calling it "middle class and bourgeois, irrelevant, and totally unaware of the real problems in society." The main problem, in his view, lay in the class structure, the stranglehold of the ruling class. "It will take more than a bunch of stoned hippies wearing bells and saying 'Right on, man' to change that," he would storm.

His thoughts were preoccupied with the class struggle. He chose not to look inward but to devote his attention to the injustices in society and the balance of power.

The Radicalizing of the Redgraves

I found myself caught in a genuinely painful dilemma. With my children growing older, I had more freedom, more time for myself. I went to underground meetings, began to develop friendships with feminists and met the challenging Australian author and professor Germaine Greer. Corin did not like these new friends at all. When I wanted to bring them home with me in the evenings, he would refuse to talk to them or would be so contemptuous of their views, my views, that he would make it quite clear that though he might listen under duress, he considered us all impotent and irrelevant.

I was furious. How dare he tell me what to think? But I was not yet strong enough to stand up to him in my own home, his home. Instead I would go to other people's houses, and try to keep the conflict away from mine. I was still under his thumb. Even though he disapproved of my political activities, relegating the liberation of women to child's play, he wanted me to go with him and attend meetings of his choice.

We attended one at Kenneth Tynan's house in Onslow Square, where Tynan's new wife, Kathy, presided in all her gracious blond elegance. The luxurious house seethed with noise and chaos.

I sat listening to boys who had gone AWOL from the American army, fled to Sweden, then escaped to smuggle themselves into England to raise money for their brothers still in hiding. They looked anxious, wearing the furtive look of people on the run. Their eloquence was born of sheer desperation.

I took in the gilt mirrors, the fashionable paintings, the expensive furniture, the sleek black cats. Then my eye caught the label on the wine that was being handed around—absolutely the cheapest you could buy in the supermarket.

"I bet they don't serve this when Sir Laurence comes to dinner," I whispered to Corin. I found the whole attitude of many of those present demeaning. It seemed to me as though the trendies were making their token gesture, doing their Good Works. The atmosphere reeked of fortunate people patronizing the less fortunate, and I didn't like the smell.

Corin and I had always lived fairly close to the bread line. I was used to vinegar in my own home, but it was not what one would expect from one of the world's most successful critics and theater producers.

Corin and I contributed what we could and left early.

We were still involved with the antinuclear movement, civil rights, and the campaign against the war in Vietnam. Vanessa was in contact with Jane Fonda, who was incurring the wrath of right wing Americans, much as Vanessa was with people in Britain, by stridently protesting the war, making speeches on campus, giving interviews and organizing the Vietnam veterans into a coherent force.

When dear Doctor Spock, on whom I had depended so thoroughly when my children were small, suddenly emerged as a civil rights leader and planned to visit England on a world tour for peace, Corin and Vanessa went into action. They organized a concert-cum-rally for him at the Lyceum Theater in London under the direction of our old friend Patrick Dromgoole and arranged to have the performance televised.

The intention was to highlight the real-life drama of man's inhumanity to man enacted across the world. Corin did much of the organizing, introduced the good doctor and the different contributors, including actress and writer Patricia Neal, who spoke movingly on human rights, and members of the Living Theater, who reenacted, with stunning accuracy, Bobby Seale's scenes in the Chicago courtroom when, charged for conspiracy with the Chicago Eight at the Democratic Convention, he was the only black man on trial and the only one to be bound hand and foot and manacled to a chair.

Vanessa had linked with Jane Fonda to bring to Europe war veterans, some of them paraplegics, who were prepared to speak out against the atrocities they had seen and been subjected to during the war. At the Spock concert, she gave a brief speech of introduction for them and then left the men to speak for themselves with the eloquence of unvarnished truth.

The Radicalizing of the Redgraves

The protests against the war grew.

One cold Sunday, Corin, Vanessa and I joined a demonstration where one hundred thousand people marched across London, glad to brave the elements for their beliefs. We marched with solidarity, joined by a common cause. However, there is a paranoid belief among all the members of the radical Left that they were being watched all the time by either the police, the Special Branch, the FBI, the CIA or BOSS. On this particular march, as we walked arm in arm, linked like a great gray serpent across the park, chanting "Ho, Ho, Ho Chi Minh," a young policeman broke ranks and walked straight up to one of our number and addressed him by name.

Immediately the line froze. Was it possible that every policeman in England really did know every left wing demonstrator by name? We were all shocked.

" 'Ullo, mate," said the policeman, grabbing a nearby lapel. "Remember me? We was at school together."

The sigh of relief could be heard halfway across London.

For years Corin refused to make important telephone calls from our flat, and there was little doubt that our number was tapped after Corin and Vanessa became so publicly controversial.

In the underground magazine *Oz*, a number was published which you could ring to check whether your own line was tapped. First you dialed three digits, which they gave you, and then the last four of your own number. There was then a recorded voice which said, "Testing, testing, testing." When you put the receiver down that number would then return your call, if your line was free of interference. If there was no return call, it meant you were being bugged.

For months we shrugged off the fact that the number never rang back, persuading ourselves that it was probably a typically inefficient piece of misinformation from the underground network. Eventually Corin decided we should change the number. Of course, I made the check call immediately after. To my immense relief, for the first time ever, there was a response—the welcome sound of ringing.

One week later I called again. I waited and waited for the reassuring ring to tell me I was safe from the all-hearing ears of the police or the Secret Service or whoever the hell it was who was listening to our most private and personal conversations. It did not come.

It upset me for days.

It was after the Vietnam war protest demonstration that culminated in Grosvenor Square and left bruised and beaten bodies in the wake of panicking police horses, the demonstration in which Vanessa strode at the head of the huge column of protestors, valiantly urging them on as she flung herself into the fray ahead of them, that I really began to feel afraid of the public disapproval of the Redgrave family.

In our move to Coleherne Court we had carried over our old phone number, which was still listed in the directory under Vanessa's name. Suddenly the anonymous phone calls started seriously intruding into our lives. Up until then they had been an occasional nuisance, which worried me more than Corin. Now they started to shrill into our home at the rate of one every three minutes. The venom shocked me.

Vanessa's publicity after the Grosvenor Square riots had reactivated people's interest in her. The callers would assume I was Vanessa and start suggesting the most degrading sexual perversions imaginable. Or else they threatened immediate death, not only to me, but also my children, probably assuming that they were Vanessa's.

I was jerked back into remembering a horrible period, just after Luke's birth, when after an announcement in the paper about our new child, I was suddenly deluged with poison-pen letters saying things like "A curse on you and your brats," and "All Redgraves are whores."

When I told Vee about it, she told me never to read letters like that.

"The minute that you realize it is a poison-pen letter," she said, "put it down immediately. If you read on, the disgusting threats and abuse somehow stick in your mind, no matter how crazy you know the people are who write them."

I began to long for anonymity. We eventually made our telephone number ex-directory, but I was well aware that although the phone no longer threatened, the hatred was still there.

15

Vanessa

In late 1967 I began to visit Vanessa more frequently, seeking her advice and thoughts on the political direction her brother was beginning to take. Although people often assumed Vanessa was the force that propelled Corin politically, in actuality she was the one who followed him. In those days she felt as I did, that an alternative consciousness was worth a try. Like me, she smoked dope and, unlike me, had experimented with acid and found it more pleasing than had her brother.

Sometimes Vee and I would spend weekends alone at Odiham with just the children, bottles of chilled champagne for company, talking through the night and taking long walks in the beautiful countryside, trying to sort out and understand the changes that were happening to both of us. Vee's changes had been bigger than mine: 1967 was the year of her divorce from Tony Richardson.

Her marriage had folded. Like a pack of glossy cards, the house that Vee built had tumbled down around her. Vanessa had adored her husband. They had been creative equals. His reputation as a director preceded him as her reputation as an actress preceded her. They were the golden couple, naturals for the title of first lady and gentleman of the stage once occupied by Vivien Leigh and Laurence Olivier.

In 1962, when they married, Tony was directing *Tom Jones.* It was one of the best British movies of the decade and made Tony not only a rich man but a highly acclaimed and sought-after film director. This was a departure for him. Previously he had made only one film, John Osborne's *Look Back in Anger,* and he was better known as a stage director.

Woodfall Films, the new company he started with John Osborne, hailed as the vanguard of the British New Wave, had produced and financed *The Loneliness of the Long Distance Runner.* This was a film about the final defiance of the individual against the system. Tony decided to star Tom Courtenay, until then a virtually unknown actor, on whom he was prepared, with his unerring eye for stalking new talent, to take the risk of letting a major film ride. Michael Redgrave played the head of the Borstal detention school to which Courtenay was committed.

Michael's previous film image had been that of the matinee idol, a distinguished, middle-aged heartthrob. He was also well known as a character actor. He had always acted in films produced by the old established studios. Having conquered the traditional stage and mastered the techniques of Shakespearean acting, playing what he described as "all the heroes," Michael now enjoyed working with the avant-garde. He had always held left wing views, had voted for the Labor Party, and at one time was sympathetic to the extreme Left. He was revitalized by working with people who were connected with change, both artistic and political.

Tony's next venture was directing Laurence Olivier in Osborne's *The Entertainer.* It was during the filming that Olivier first met Joan Plowright, who was cast as his wife.

Tony was flying high in the critics' esteem. His film *A Taste of Honey,* with Rita Tushingham, a friend of Lynn's, received rave reviews. Rita was proclaimed an overnight star. Tony could do no wrong. But as so often happens, the critics seemed to be longing for an opportunity to shoot down the idol that they themselves had helped create. Although he had proved himself, they could not wait for him to behave like a fool and overstep their mark of appreciation. The trouble began for Tony when he started his collaboration with the renowned French actress Jeanne Moreau.

Jeanne Moreau was an ageless femme fatale. Brought to the attention of English filmgoers by her performance in Truffaut's *Jules and Jim* and *Moderato Cantabile*, the latter with Jean-Paul Belmondo, her boldly sensual features were by now internationally known. She was a younger, modern version of the powerful French actress Simone Signoret, and Tony was fascinated by her.

She combined intellect and passion. She appeared independent and invulnerable, but suggested the possibility of total subjection should a man strike the right chord. She was beautiful, but not in the glossy Hollywood way. Flawed, fearless of showing the lines of life in her face, she destroyed forever the idea that to be desirable you have to be twenty and blond, with a big chest and skinny legs. She was small, curved, soft, desirable. She was moody, wore no makeup, and walked arrogantly and confidently through the ranks of younger and more obviously beautiful women. She epitomized the liberated woman, caring little for superficial image, while subtly suggesting ecstasy to any man male enough to conquer her.

I can remember Vee telling me of how Tony first met Jeanne at lunch.

"He came back literally elated," she said. "It frightens me because I recognize that feeling. I've felt it myself. She must be extraordinary—Tony seemed transformed, set alight. He is going to do a series of films with her. He has never done that with me."

She sounded rueful and a little sad.

Tony's first film with Jeanne was called *Mademoiselle*, from a strange, erotic script by Jean Genet. It appealed to Tony because of its bizarre and macabre interpretation of the games men and women play with each other. A master of mind games himself,

Tony was always drawn to the perverse and hidden sides of human nature.

There is a scene in *Mademoiselle* where Moreau, playing a rather prim schoolmistress in a French provincial village, falls in love with an Italian immigrant woodcutter and throws herself at his feet, kissing his shadow as though she were touching every crevice of his body. In fact she never actually touches him at all. Some audiences were so embarrassed by this primitive sensuality that they laughed derisively, unable to handle the raw passion.

The fact that he could evoke such a performance from his star and put on film such subtle but ferocious sensuality spoke volumes of their feelings for each other.

Vanessa was understandably hurt by Tony's involvement with Jeanne, and it was not long after this difficult period in their lives that they separated. They had shared many happy times together and were both devoted to their two children, but career demands had caused too many long separations. They saw each other so seldom; their interests diverged. They spent time with other people. Their family life was always being disrupted, an inborn hazard of show business.

The breakup of any relationship is always painful, particularly for the one left behind. Vanessa was devastated. She, as a great actress, had always managed to maintain a facade of near indifference for the outside world, masking her vulnerability. But for the first time she was visibly unhappy. She was hurt; she was jealous of Jeanne; and I think it was only her career and her devotion to her children that helped her ride out the wave of sorrow.

Morgan—A Suitable Case for Treatment had opened to ecstatic reviews. Both she and the film were a dazzling success. Vanessa, the serious Shakespearean darling of the drama critics, had moved on to new horizons and was suddenly being hailed as the most beautiful, talented and attractive film star in England. Such praise served to boost her self-confidence at a time when she badly needed it and to heighten her already glowing beauty.

Almost every man who saw the film came away a little in love with her. She was delighted. She had always felt that she was too large, too tall, and too overpowering to men. Now her image was that of a sensuous woman. The quality that set her aside and above her rivals was that her clear intelligence shone through. But, for a change, men did not find that threatening: they found her alluring.

She began to be courted by all the top photographers. Norman Parkinson did an entire television documentary around her. He used her as an exotic model; he filmed her lying draped on sofas in sumptuous dresses, looking just about as far removed from her previous image of blue-stockinged Shakespearean actress as a thistle from a rose.

She blossomed as her career blossomed, looking more beautiful than she ever had. She exchanged her glasses for contact lenses and told me this was the first time she had ever been able to see her unadorned face clearly. She had either seen it with glasses on or else blurred. Now she could have fun experimenting with makeup on her eyes, quite her most beautiful feature. The effect was astounding, and finally she knew it and began to enjoy her own beauty in a way I don't think she ever had before. She began to gain an independence I'd never seen in her; out of adversity, she was carving a new life for herself. It seemed full of glamour and the promise of new relationships. From my vantage point, under the nappy basket, it looked very inviting!

In 1965, Antonioni's *Blow-Up* was also a great success for Vanessa, and she became notorious for the scene in which she calmly removed her shirt. At the time it was considered appropriately outrageous. Something that "serious actresses" did not do, but swingers did.

I remember that on the rare occasions I saw her during that period, she was utterly exhausted. She was appearing in the play *The Prime of Miss Jean Brodie* at night and shooting *Blow-Up* all day. She left for the studios in the early morning, often before dawn, and worked until it was time for a chauffeur to drive her to the theater in time for her performance. Both roles were very demanding, and she began to fear that she would forget her lines on stage. She told me that playing *Jean Brodie* became such a nightmare for her that it was three years before she could face the thought of acting in the theater again, and then only in the provinces in a Manchester production of *Daniel Deronda*.

Although Vanessa was essentially terribly serious, there was an almost girlish side to her that was innocent almost to the point of naiveté. Sometimes she and I would read through the Hollywood glitter magazines, amused by the trivial gossip about who was dating whom, who was starring in what. She read them as if she were totally unaware of the fact that she was a great star herself. She behaved as if all these people belonged in another, more glamorous world than hers, as if she had no part in it—as if no matter how much acclaim she received, she could not really believe that the everyday Vee was the same person who appeared at Oscar ceremonies and premieres and whom people were moved to applaud when they saw her in the cinema. Yet sometimes we would go to the movies together and people would not even recognize her, perhaps because she projects so little of the film star image, and somehow keeps the force of her personality for the screen or stage alone.

When she and Tony separated, she continued to live in their house in St. Peter's Square, Chiswick. Tony wanted to leave it in trust for the children and for Vee to use it until such time as the kids were old enough to want it for themselves. Her private life had moved far from the bright lights and the social scene. She bothered little with public appearances.

Later, when she fell in love again, she was to move to another house in the same square so as not to act out a new love affair against an old background steeped in memories.

It was not until the late seventies that she bought the small, anonymous little terraced brick house where she now lives in Hammersmith. But her personal choice of lifestyle has always been unpretentious, bordering on plain.

In all the time I knew her, Vanessa's car was functional, and her clothes functional as well. They needed to be. She would work twenty-four hours a day if she could. The work ethic ruled her life. Be it a play, a film or a cause, she put her entire energy into it.

She is a woman without vanity, a rare quality in any human being. Many times she told me with astonishment of the men who had (to me, understandably) fallen madly in love with her.

"At the Oscar ceremony," she told me, "Jon Voight whispered in my ear that he had loved me for years!"

She was clearly delighted, but she laughed like a disbelieving child; since she did not play the game of seductress, she was almost oblivious of her powers to enchant.

One evening over dinner, during a break in her filming of Ken Russell's *The Devils,* she confided that Oliver Reed had also admitted that he was smitten by her.

"Oh, Vee," I groaned, "I have always had a soft spot for him. You have them all, you could at least leave Oliver for me!"

Another time she told me that when she was filming in Italy with Tinto Brass, the director, they were alone one day in the viewing room watching rushes. "He went up to the screen and traced the pattern of my lips with his finger. Then he kissed them," she said, genuinely astonished, and quite moved.

I wasn't surprised to hear such tales. She has the appeal of a pre-Raphaelite woman. Slightly distanced from obvious sexuality, and despite her height, which she feels makes her awkward, Vee is magnetically attractive in a dreamlike way.

She is completely uncompetitive as a woman, and her stories of the men who pursued her were never meant to be boastful. There is no bitchiness in her at all, which does not mean that she has no edge—she does, but as in her brother's case, this has more to do with not suffering fools gladly.

She reached new heights of international stardom when she went to America to play Guinevere in the film version of *Camelot,* already a successful stage musical. Until her arrival on the scene, Julie Andrews, the stage's Guinevere, was the English queen of Hollywood, but Julie's brand of nice-girl-next-door appeal was no match for Vanessa's mystery and fire.

It was during the filming of *Camelot* that she fell in love with the handsome young Italian actor Franco Nero, who had shipped himself off to Hollywood on the strength of his success in the new milieu of "spaghetti Westerns," which were then creating an entire new movie empire in Rome.

Hot on the heels of Clint Eastwood's sudden ascent to fame following his role in *A Fistful of Dollars*, a low-budget Italian movie directed by Sergio Leone, Franco emerged as one of the best-looking answers to the Hollywood glamour boys.

Vanessa arrived in Hollywood fresh from her success in *Morgan* and *Blow-Up*. Inevitably she was caught in the net thrown out for the catch of the season. Warren Beatty, with his reputation for pursuing not just beautiful women, but particularly the favorite of the moment and preferably European, proved Vee's susceptibility to a handsome face, quick charm and pioneering spirit.

But even in the teeth of Beatty's competition, Franco fulfilled his role as Lancelot, the knight in shining armor, and captured the love of his Lady Guinevere, both on screen and off. They had an intense affair in Los Angeles which heightened the passion on screen enormously, and it was no surprise that when the film was finished they returned to Europe to live together.

Although there had been a relationship or two for Vee since her separation from Tony, including a whirlwind romance with George Hamilton (who was taking time off from his demanding role as Lynda Bird Johnson's escort) Franco was the first man Vanessa had wanted to introduce into the bosom of her family.

Corin and I spent many weekends at Odiham with Franco and Vanessa, then in the first throes of their romance. My children adored Franco because he constantly acted out for them every screen hero he had ever played, or wished to play, from gunslinger to Robin Hood. He made bows and arrows from the trees in the nearby woods and spent hours reliving the heroic roles as my children darted from tree to tree, acting in turn the Merry Men of Sherwood, King Arthur's enemies and poor Mexican peasants. Franco never tired of those games, and the three of them would slump back to the cottage, exhausted but happy, to confront Corin and Vanessa, who were busy writing speeches to be delivered to one radical group or another, miles removed from childhood frolics, although not yet embroiled in the Workers Revolutionary Party led by Gerry Healey.

Franco was both fascinated and infuriated by Vee's independent spirit and her determined political involvement. In Italy, the woman is expected to bear children, take care of her man's every need, cook spaghetti, and Franco's expectations were traditional. He was threatened by the politics that involved Vee when she was not working. In order to make him feel more at ease, she became an expert Italian cook, making the dough for his pasta herself. She stretched her homemaking talents to the limit in taking care of his needs, but refused to give up her identity. It was the cause of many arguments between them.

One evening Franco invited us to join him and Vanessa for dinner at the fashionable Arethusa Restaurant. It quickly became clear that Franco was not in a good mood.

"Look over there, Vanessa," he said, as we were seated at our table. "Take a good look. There is a really beautiful woman, a real woman. Look how she smiles at her man, look how she is dressed, she knows how to please a man, she knows what a man wants in a woman, not like you."

He glared across the table at Vanessa, to make sure his words were having the effect he wished.

I was horrified. The woman Franco was praising—the first of many during the evening—had all the seductive powers of a Kewpie doll. Her makeup was perfect, her hair untouchable, her expression blank, her clothes expensive and fashionable, but lacking flair or originality. How could Franco insult Vee by such odious comparisons?

Matters got worse. The night before, Maggie Smith had won an Oscar for her film performance in *The Prime of Miss Jean Brodie*, the role that Vanessa had created so brilliantly on stage. In fact, I thought Vee's performance was altogether more interesting, and the play more touching than the film. But Franco decided to use Maggie's new trophy as his new line of attack.

"That Maggie Smith is a real actress," Franco intoned with the pompous air of one who knows. "She doesn't waste her time on politics like you, Vanessa. She works hard. It is quite right that she should get an Oscar. You never will. She deserves it. She was wonderful as Miss Jean Brodie. Wonderful. Not like you. She is a great actress." Vanessa was near tears.

I felt angry, but I knew that Franco simply could not begin to understand Vanessa—as I had not for so many years. To understand that although she loved him and had borne him a son, Carlo, she still had other, equally powerful commitments in her life. She was elusive. He could never quite encompass her, own her, contain her. That hurt his pride, and he was irrationally jealous. He wanted to destroy the aura of self-containment, the poised, aristocratic aloofness that both she and Corin so often projected and was so infuriating to people trying to reach them.

This time he succeeded. We left the restaurant with Vanessa in tears and Corin shouting at him to leave his sister alone.

Opposites are often attracted to each other, but it had become clear that the days of the "spaghetti Western" star and the heroine of Stratford-on-Avon were numbered.

Vanessa's commitment to politics was underestimated by Franco, I thought. Perhaps, like so many others, he didn't take her seriously. There were those who viewed her commitment as a publicity stunt—or worse, as the ravings of a guilty, rich, successful woman, who needs to make herself into a martyr.

She hated to give interviews, and it was all the promoters of her films could do to get her to speak to the press at all.

Guilt may have driven her, perhaps because she was born into a privileged lifestyle. But whatever lay behind the political rhetoric, I believed, for those first ten years that I knew her, that here was a remarkably powerful woman, prepared to dedicate her life to improving the human condition in a world riddled with inconsistencies and inequality.

Unfortunately, politics eventually drove an immovable wedge between Vanessa and me, as it did between Corin and me. In the beginning I admired the fact that rather than rest on her theatrical laurels and enjoy a life of luxury, she chose to live by the socialist maxim of "a simple life." But as the politics became fanatical and began to rule her, I changed my view.

My sister-in-law is a woman who could have ruled over any world she chose. And, with her characteristic disregard for convention, theatrical or any other kind, she chose to use her strength as an actress to convince people not of the magic of the theater, but of the passion of revolutionary politics.

But that is to come. In the days before she became so radical and we grew apart, we had a good time raising our children together and warming to each other as friends—jumping into her car to go to a late-night movie, planning our liberation from two thousand years of male chauvinism, babysitting for each other and dining together—as often as her work schedule would allow.

Until Corin introduced Vanessa to the Workers Revolutionary Party, ours was a fairly normal sisterly friendship. By the early seventies, that had all changed.

16

The Sorcerer and Black Power

As the rest of the world became more and more aware of the Redgrave family affiliations with radical causes, so each of us learned to handle the aggression leveled at us by critics. Although my husband and his sister were well used to such situations, I can vividly remember how difficult I found it to remain level-headed while under attack from people I had never seen before and probably never would again.

For the first time I realized how politics could so passionately divide people against their own kind, and certainly against people who in any way set themselves up as targets. Although Rachel and Michael supported us loyally, by the late sixties and early seventies all three of us, Corin, Vanessa and I, were on the firing line. In my case that sometimes meant attack even from my own family. I would find myself at smart London parties where perfect strangers would come up to me slightly pickled and totally incensed once they heard that my name was Redgrave.

"So you're married to that Redgrave boy, are you?" said these upright Tories, rigid in their armor of social status and right wing principles. "Leftie, are you? Bloody reds, I'd say. Bunch of bloody commies! Believe in all that rubbish about power to the working classes, do you? Want to take over the world I shouldn't wonder. Want to hand us over to the Russkies."

"Of course not." I would attempt to placate them, looking around the room crowded with cocktail-filled and very hostile guests. I'd begin by gently trying to explain the ideals held by my husband and particularly my sister-in-law, who was always much more public in her defense of minority causes—and who in their eyes had toppled from grace by ignoring the age-old traditions of grand actresses of the theater by stepping off her pedestal and marching among the proletariat.

But it never worked. These upholders of the Establishment could not open their minds long enough to listen. They did not want to hear about the dangers of fascism, or the sense of socialism. They simply wanted to attack.

Sometimes their vitriol would so upset me that I would have to leave, frustrated that their views had the same relevance as a herd of dinosaurs in this day and age.

"People are so afraid for their own structures," I told Corin, "for their own security, so anxious to continue living in a familiar world that they attack even before they defend—and the attacks are vicious!"

"Why are you surprised?" was his response. "Don't you know that there will be vast changes in the system in the very near future and that although capitalists know that they will, as Marx predicted, attempt to resist their own downfall, in doing so they will bring about their own destruction. The right wing knows it, even if you don't, and they're afraid. No wonder."

He sounded grim. I knew that for as long as he had been reading Marx as a political analyst he had believed that the overall pattern in history would be that inevitably the lower classes would rise against the rulers in a deadly confrontation.

Corin's energy was simmering. Like Vanessa, he needed causes, and like Vanessa the next arena he was drawn into was that of Black Power. In the battle of Black versus White he jumped into the ring, ready to pull on the boxing gloves himself in defense of his black brothers.

By now our political life was almost completely entwined with our social life. We spent time mostly with people who thought and felt that flowers and bells and kisses were no longer strong enough protest against the injustices of the world and the encroachments of capitalism. Corin felt there were things to do and that I should do them with him. I was prepared to go with him as far as I could. Inevitably that meant we saw a great deal of Vanessa the rare times she was not working. It was at one of these occasions that she introduced us to a black writer she had brought with her from America.

Corin and I were at a party given by film director Silvio Narizzano, who years previously had directed Lynn in *Georgy Girl*. He lived in a sumptuous flat, full of gilt mirrors and velvety carpets, and as Corin and I stood there sipping champagne and chatting, the world of politics seemed light years away.

It was hard to miss Vanessa's entrance: she swept in, tall and blond and striking, on the arm of an equally tall, arrogant black American wearing a large medallion bearing the image of Malcolm X around his neck.

As Vanessa moved toward us to introduce her companion, I could see him looking around the room with barely concealed contempt.

"Meet Hakim Jamal," said Vee, in her low, thrilling voice, as though she were introducing us to God. "Hakim is a friend of mine from America. We met through Jean Seberg, who is involved with the Black Panthers, and he wanted to come to England to find out what was happening in the Black Power movement over here, so I've invited him to stay with me and I *know* you and Corin will be much better able to fill him in on the details of different people and organizations than I am. . . ."

In fact, Vee's active involvement with black groups came before ours, although since living in America and going through Harlem, we had been sensitive to the problems of black people in England, aware of the prejudice against blacks in schools and jobs, as the problems of undereducation and unemployment became more pronounced.

I knew instantly that this exotic stranger was to have a powerful effect on our lives. It wasn't just that he held in check a force which I felt could be let loose precisely when he chose, or that from the first second his eyes had a hypnotic beam, or even that I knew Corin was looking for something specific to do in the black movement. It was a flash of clairvoyance, like a spider running up my spine, which happened to me very seldom but with deadly accuracy. The last time I could remember feeling it was the first time I saw Corin on stage at the Royal Court.

Hakim noticed that Corin had a book sticking out of his pocket. This wasn't unusual; it was a rather endearing manifestation of absent-mindedness. Hakim's eagle eyes missed nothing. He could see the title from where he was, and the minute he realized it was Alex Haley's biography of Malcolm X, his face lit up and he was immediately eager to engage us in conversation.

"Malcolm X is a cousin of mine," he said, leaning toward me conspiratorially. "He helped to cure me of heroin addiction." The need for alcohol and drugs, it turned out, had been replaced in Hakim by a gnawing, unshakable hatred for the white man.

"I have come to Europe to confirm my view that the white man is the devil." The man paused and looked at us all steadily. "Wherever he is on the face of the earth."

Vanessa looked a little stunned and I wasn't surprised. If he thought white men were devils, why take help from the devil? Obviously Vanessa had brought him over here under her protective wing as yet another cause.

All three of us were quite ready and equal to rise to his challenge, but he had a masterly use of speech and a quiet, urgent manner that allowed us to believe we were exceptions to his rule. Even then we were being seduced.

As a pair, he and Vanessa made a strong physical impact on the group of champagne-tipsy guests, although no one wanted to plunge themselves into the polemics of racism with this stranger. I was aware that even Vanessa's fellow actors and actresses, people who freely admired her art and respected her work, were reluctant to engage her in conversation for fear of its turning into a political harangue. With reason—I had often seen and heard it happen. Especially because it became quite clear that Hakim was incapable of holding a conversation that did not highlight the plight of black people all over the world.

So, linking arms, the Redgrave group decided to leave and make a party of their own.

The four of us had dinner together. We listened to Hakim, whose voice was an almost uninterrupted accompaniment to the clatter of hungry diners.

"My people been stamped on too long," he said angrily. "It's time for a change. And if it don't happen peacefully, then we'll use violence."

We did not believe in using arms of any kind, or *I* certainly didn't. If there was to be a revolution in the streets I didn't want to see blood spilled and bombs thrown through windows. But then, I didn't grow up in poor, black America.

Neither did Corin or Vanessa for that matter. Vanessa's sympathy with Black Power began when she had met Hakim while he was speaking at a rally to raise money for a children's school named after Malcolm X. Vanessa's friend Jean Seberg, then actively committed to the Black Panthers, who was also part of the fund-raising committee, had introduced them.

"He is in great demand as an orator," said Vee, fixing enormous eyes on him with admiration. "You really should hear him speak."

We did. He transfixed us all. He had a flair for rhetoric and a spellbinding intensity that caught us in a vortex of excitement. By the end of the evening Corin and I had been as firmly sucked into his net as Vanessa before us.

Vanessa, of course, was off again within days. She had work to do, she said, another film. Could Corin and I please be hospitable to her friend Hakim? Show him something of London? Take him to meet any of the Black Power people we knew?

I had been through this before with Vanessa. I called it the "I'll just drop my latest revolutionary on your doorstep" pattern. Of course I could have refused. But Corin was keen to find out more about what was happening in America, and I neither wanted to stir things up between Corin and Vanessa nor did I really want to turn down the opportunity of knowing this peculiarly compelling man.

Perhaps, as Corin had said all those years ago in Harlem, there might really be something active we could do for black people in this country, and perhaps it was Hakim who would show us the way.

So Hakim Jamal spent a great deal of time with us at Coleherne Court during the three weeks left on the budget return ticket that Vanessa had given him. It was as though he threw a sorcerer's cloak around us, so magnetically were we all three drawn to one another. Corin and I completely fell for his combination of passion and humor.

We took him out to dinner one evening. I was getting soaked to the skin because I had holes in my shoes, and quietly grumbling to myself as I moved from puddle to puddle. Hakim turned on me in an absolute fury, shouting that I was lucky to have socks on my feet, let alone shoes—some people had nothing.

It didn't even occur to me to point out that his shoes had perfectly good leather soles and *we* had just taken *him* out to dinner.

He even had me feeling shamefaced about having a poster of Jimi Hendrix hanging in my lavatory, saying Hendrix didn't look black because it was a psychedelic poster in oranges and greens and he looked more like a Martian than a black man. He said I ought to have more pictures of black people around so that my children would grow up in the right atmosphere.

Silly me, thinking I had racially integrated walls, and not noticing Jimi Hendrix was flaming orange.

But then Hakim was the one who shrank away from kissing my daughter goodnight, saying he "couldn't bear to touch white skin."

Nevertheless, when Hakim flew away to America at the end of three weeks, he had left his mark. He had turned us on to the cause of Black Power. He had encouraged us to work with some of the black organizations springing up in London, people who were trying to help the poor black communities with their legal rights, their housing, the schooling of their children.

Corin and I decided it was time for us to see if there was anything we could do that would really help. We didn't have enough money to make grand gestures, like buying schools or houses for those in need, which Vanessa did much later on, but we could help raise money for them; we could, through our contacts, find lawyers for people who needed them, and we could help organize bookshops, community arts centers and nursery facilities for those who desperately needed such services.

It was at this time that we first met Michael X, a clever and manipulative black leader, who had picked up on the emergence of the black movement in London and was capitalizing on it brilliantly. He was a West Indian, and he knew that West Indians in the city angrily felt that they were being deprived of many of their legal rights. Michael decided he would take up their cause, articulate their needs and catch the attention of the media. Which he did.

What no one realized then was that his previous claim to fame had been the efficient handling of call girls, slum properties and illicit drugs. But as Corin and I moved among the black communities we did discover that most of them feared and despised Michael X.

It was 1969. The black movement had spread to Europe in the wake of Eldridge Cleaver's flight from the racial war in America. Black Panthers were being busted with a savagery seemingly reserved by the American police for black people. The latest bulletin reported that after surrounding a Panther hideout for three days, the police stormed the house and in the resulting shoot-out all the Panthers were killed. There were no police casualties. Cleaver went into exile, holding court in Tangiers. We occasionally heard of movement organizers in London being slipped in to see him.

Suddenly London was forced into awareness of coming violence. Revolution was getting serious. A flower in the barrel of the gun was only pretty as long as the gun remained silent. With the Watts riots and the deaths of Martin Luther King and Malcolm X, it was impossible to ignore the fact that there was no longer a peace movement. Protest meant danger. Especially for blacks.

In London, Corin took part in a demonstration by the West Indian community in Notting Hill Gate. Nine West Indian men were busted at the Mangrove Restaurant, to this day a key black community center. They were demonstrating by carrying pigs' heads on sticks as a symbol of their constant oppression and harassment by the Notting Hill police.

It was all getting much more violent than we could ever have imagined in the summer of love when we were gamboling in the woods with our flowers and our joss sticks. This was not souls on ice, but souls on fire.

One of the ways we were able to help was by raising bail for black people who had been busted for little or no reason. When one of our friends was arrested by the police in late 1969 for distributing "incendiary and subversive" literature, he was refused bail and incarcerated in Brixton jail.

Fortunately we had access to one of England's finest barristers, playwright John Mortimer, who managed to secure our friend his temporary freedom by at least getting him out on bail. We hoped he could win the case on the grounds of his being deprived of his civil liberties, although unfortunately that was only a naive hope. The four hundred dollars of our savings that Corin and I invested in the case was lost.

Still, one of my best memories of those times was the party given for us by a black group at an old house in Stoke Newington on the outskirts of London. They wanted to thank us for our help, and since they didn't have money, they gave us hospitality.

I was nervous. Corin and I had never before been the only white people in the room, but we were instantly and overwhelmingly made to feel at home.

There was drink, smoke, spicy succulent West Indian food to warm us. I ate myself silly and danced all night. We finally left, happy and exhausted, in the small hours of the morning and drove past the forbidding tower blocks, the dilapidated houses. I was almost affronted to see how suddenly the poverty gave way to neat shop windows, fancy boutiques, expensive houses and opulence. I knew from experience that behind those doors was more loneliness than could ever be found in the grim shelters of the West Indian community.

"Money just seems to bring isolation," I said to Corin as we drove sleepily home. "Where did it all go wrong?"

At the end of the year, Hakim Jamal arrived back in London for his second visit a changed man. No longer did he say of white people that they had "stringy hair, thin lips and forked tongues." He had been having a passionate affair with Vanessa's old friend Jean Seberg. The experience had whetted his appetite for white women, and his lust knew no bounds. Within days of being back in London, he had embarked on a series of affairs with women I knew, bouncing from one to the other like a Ping-Pong ball, and he even told one of them that what he had really come back to England for was to "take Corin's wife away from him."

I found Hakim changed in other ways, too. He talked endlessly of his friendship with Marlon Brando, did nothing but drop famous names, and made it clear that he was being accepted in white society because he was a talented writer—and because women fell for him, hook, line and sinker.

In fact, he had written a book called *From the Dead Level*, about his life with Malcolm X, which had been quite well received. With his one gold earring and mocking eyes, he was the kind of brigand that women fell in love with. One of them was Gail Benson, Jonathan's divorced wife.

My long-time suitor and stalwart ally, Jonathan Benson, had married Gail four years earlier. Corin was best man, and it healed a breach that had existed between us all since Corin and I had married. Gail was quite beautiful, and much younger than Jonathan, very self-willed, original and extremely lively, with a strong mind of her own. She and Jonathan separated several times during the years they were married, and by the time Gail met Hakim they were divorced, although they still saw each other often and were close friends.

She found in Hakim the perfect man, or so she told me—a rebel, a traveler, an adventurer like herself.

However, Gail became not only his lover but his disciple. She worshipped him. For her he was the source of all energy. When he moved into her flat, the seeds of her terrible, final destruction were sown.

By the time they moved to Trinidad together, he had brainwashed her into genuinely believing he was God. We heard through Jonathan, who still kept in touch with Gail because he was worried about her, that she and Hakim had joined a commune run by Michael X.

"The trouble is," Corin pointed out, "if Gail thinks Hakim is God and Michael X thinks Michael X is God, then what is Hakim going to do? There's going to be a serious conflict of interests, I'd say. I only hope they aren't both so power-hungry that Gail gets caught in the middle of a fight."

It wasn't exactly what happened, but Gail was the one to suffer. We later learned, through Jonathan and the newspapers, that Gail was terribly shocked by having to confront the idea that it was not Hakim but Michael X who was God. She *wanted* to believe Hakim was God. She had just given up her home, friends and family for Hakim because she had believed he was divine.

She determined to find proof for Hakim that Michael X was not God, to show him up as a fraud. She was pretty sure there were some odd goings-on at the commune.

She waited until Michael was out, and twice crept into his room to rifle his papers for incriminating evidence to show her lover. Twice she was caught. That was enough for Michael to pronounce his sentence upon her. The death sentence. God had spoken. His judgment would be carried out by others. . . .

Early one morning, while Michael and Hakim were out for a drive in the countryside, she was led by Michael's henchmen to a shallow grave on the commune's grounds.

"Do you know who this is for?" they asked her.

"Of course not," she replied innocently.

"It's for you," they said.

When she tried to run they attacked her with machetes. It was revealed at her autopsy that she had put up a strong struggle, had fought them for as long as her strength held out. It also revealed that she had been buried alive. Earth was found in her intestines.

Shortly after Gail's death, Hakim was shot dead in Boston by a militant black group called the Mau Mau, named after the terrorist secret society in Kenya.

Corin had once described Hakim as "the lone alley cat of black politics." That is how he died. Alone, in an alley.

Michael was eventually brought to trial. He was sentenced to death, not for Gail's murder—she had been killed on his orders but not by his hand—but for the murder of one of his own black brothers.

When Kate Millett, the feminist author, telephoned one day to ask for our support in trying to get Michael X off the hook at his trial, I was appalled. She wanted us to say that he had been a victim of white racist society, of the horrors of British imperialism.

I suggested that if she really wanted to find out what kind of a man Michael X was she talk to some of his own people in the West Indian communities of London. Even his own people, I told her, knew him to be an evil charlatan with no scruples and fewer principles.

My heart was no longer in radical politics. There was too much sham, too much carelessness, too much hype, too much self-aggrandizement.

17

Invasion of the Marx Brothers

Confronted by the tragedy of Gail's death, Corin withdrew. Never a man to choose head-on collision with emotion of any kind, he, not surprisingly, found a way to intellectualize all the dark feelings of doubt and guilt the murder had stirred up. In retrospect, it seems clear that the methods we each chose to deal with the murder indicated the later, more profound split.

I was content to turn inward for solace, to my home and children, trying to make sense of the outside world by ordering my inside world. Corin clung more and more to radical politics. He started to go to the meetings of an extreme left wing group called the Socialist Labor League, later to become the Workers Revolutionary Party. Many artists and intellectuals who, like Corin and Vee, had mobilized people against the war in Vietnam, minority oppression and racism, were shopping around the extreme left wing to find an organization they could relate to, the tenets of which might help them make sense of the chaos they saw around them.

The Socialist Labor League seemed to offer Corin just such a degree of sanity. Far from being put off by the rhetoric, he was drawn to the structure and discipline.

A talented young actress named Kika Markham took him to that first meeting. She was appearing with him in a play and she and some of her friends had already belonged to the group for a while. Like Corin, she had been drawn to the Left from a young age, and while still in her teens had lived with radical English playwright David Mercer. Her father, actor David Markham, was well known for his activities in freeing political prisoners. She was not afraid to live out her own beliefs.

A group such as the Socialist Labor League draws in people whenever and however it can. Corin was attracted to the rigid discipline imposed by its secretary and leader, Gerry Healey. Corin is a pragmatist. He wanted not simply another cause, another idea, but something concrete to do. Healey offered a revolution Corin could both believe in intellectually and work for on a day-to-day basis. Healey convinced him that through the League he would be part of the overthrow of the government and the creation of a new society.

As Corin said to me, "I am not black, I am not American, I am not Jewish, and I am not a Greek poet. I must try to change things from my stance as a white middle-class intellectual."

For people who felt as he did and who had already been involved in causes like the Vietnam protest movement, Black Power, and overthrowing the oppressive regime of the Greek junta, there were three main parties with which they might affiliate: the Socialist Labor League, the International Socialists—later to become the Socialist Workers Party—and the International Marxist Group.

Corin had chosen the most puritan and disciplined structure he could find.

Once he met Healey, a brutally powerful, dynamic and charismatic man, Corin's allegiance was given. He spent endless amounts of time with Healey, who night after night came around to our flat, always accompanied by a comrade from the Party, never alone. Healey talked for hours, mixing the same dynamics of flattery and threat that Hakim had done.

I could see that Corin had chosen his side.

Healey made Corin feel he had a crucial and urgent role to play if he would commit himself *now*. The revolution would not be in ten years time or twenty, but *tomorrow*. And Healey's group was "the only one that truly supported the working classes." Corin's imagination was caught. I also believe that Corin and, later, Vanessa found in Healey the dominant male figure their father had never provided.

Healey's rhetoric made Corin feel like a dinner-party observer of the revolutionary scene, a dilettante, a child, in the old struggle of left wing politics against the right. Now in his sixties, Healey was an old campaigner. He was organizing strikes in the Irish docks in the thirties before Corin was born. Not interested in left wing trendies or political dilettantes, he was concerned with the realities of power politics, and with recruiting to his camp men and women who he felt would be crucially important to his campaign.

The recruitment of the rank and file, it later appeared, was left to others in the Party. The secretary addressed himself to the people of importance. Flattered, Corin was getting and liking the special treatment. He felt Healey could teach him invaluable techniques, would give him the benefit of experience. Healey was offering him power, a seductive promise. Corin, he knew, would not be content to be merely a guest at the dinner table.

I, on the other hand, still reeling from Gail's murder, was not about to be bullied or flattered into anything. I realized the potential dangers of fanaticism and was grateful I hadn't been as taken in as Gail. I wanted to share my life only with the reassuring comforts of friends and family.

Our spacious flat in Coleherne Court, with its high-ceilinged rooms, polished floorboards, potted plants, open fireplace and huge stereo system had been for several years a lodestone for London's eccentrics, a diverse set of writers, painters, musicians, astrologers, drifters and dropouts. Having, in the past, spent long hours away from home to accompany Corin in his political activities, I returned to a more social way of life, and our flat became a center for our friends again.

On a normal evening I could be found preparing a stew in the kitchen, a bottle of white wine on the table, girlfriends with feet up, regaling me with stories of their day, the children tugging at my arm for bedtime stories. In the old days Corin was usually happily engaged in conversation in the drawing room with their assorted husbands or lovers while I took care of domestic arrangements. Having tucked the children into bed, sometimes other people's children too, we would all sit around our large pine table, eat and drink, argue and laugh, enveloped in clouds of smoke, waves of music and the warm aura of kitchen lights and candles.

But work for the WRP was demanding. Gradually I became aware of how many evenings Corin was absent, of how the Party seemed to be making more demands on him than I had anticipated. The children began to notice his absence, missing the after-supper games he used to play with them, missing his goodnight kiss.

"Daddy is busy tonight," I would tell them. "Don't worry, he'll be here tomorrow," I would say hopefully, but with a sinking feeling that he wouldn't.

One weekend, Mickey, still a close friend, invited us to stay with him in the country. The grounds had a swimming pool and a tennis court and the children adored going there, so it was the perfect place for them to have a few glorious carefree summer days away from the grimy heat of the city. It would also get Corin away from the influence of the Party for a few days and give us time to talk. I delightedly accepted and told Corin when he came home from a Party meeting.

He immediately went to the telephone and called Mickey without even answering me. "I have more important things to do," he informed Mickey. "This is a time for serious action. Our halcyon days are over."

His words chilled me. "What on earth do you mean, Corin?" My stomach turned with apprehension.

"I mean, there are things I must do to prepare for the revolution," said Corin, "that are more important than playing in a rich man's garden."

"More important than playing with your own children?" I inquired bitterly.

My husband coldly answered, "I am afraid so."

I recalled one evening, early on in our marriage, when we were having dinner with John Hurt and Annette Robertson, the actress he was then married to. The four of us were talking about our dreams and ambitions.

"The most important thing in my life is my career," said John. "I won't allow anything or anybody to stand in its way."

"The most important thing in my life is my relationship with Deirdre," Corin argued. "My personal life comes before anything else."

At the time I was surprised by the vehemence of Corin's loyalty; it certainly took the loquacious John Hurt aback for a moment or two. But I knew my husband to be a man in whom personal ambition ranked low on his list of priorities, and all the energy that he later poured into politics was then directed toward home and family.

Now the change in him was definite and quite frightening. His emotions, always held in check, seemed to have been siphoned off. He was certainly allowing something to come before his family. Perhaps, I thought, this is where the Redgrave ambition, so obvious in the rest of the family, will surface in Corin—through the world of politics. For the first time I began to see that Corin's involvement with the Party could possibly pose a serious threat to our life together.

I was right to be alerted. One evening, he arrived back from a meeting with a new blueprint for our lives.

"We will no longer go to restaurants or have friends to dinner," he informed me. "I consider that bourgeois and a waste of time and money."

I didn't care about going to restaurants, but I did care about him emptying our home of friends. I loved and depended on our friends—they nourished me, especially as I spent so much time on my own. Of late only they and my children could make me laugh. "Humor," as Corin was drily to reply, "is the last bastion of the bourgeoisie."

Corin would return home from his meetings and glare so intimidatingly into the drawing room filled with people playing loud music and drinking wine that everyone was made to feel guilty for having a good time. "Trivial wastrels," he called them. His disapproval was such that his mere presence froze all activity, and my guests would depart as one.

I protested, almost in tears, at his impossible rudeness. I pointed out that he had had the same reaction when I began getting involved with the women's rights—everything was fine as long as I did things his way. If I wanted to think for myself or make my own friends or learn my own way, he objected.

Corin replied that he was incensed by the people we knew and thought they were no more than political poseurs. Once he had labeled someone as such, his invective was merciless. He accused them of dreading the working class. He was paranoid about their reaction to him and how that might influence my feelings.

He was beyond the point of wanting to listen to my defense of my friends, beyond the point, as far as I could see, of caring about my feelings or thoughts at all. Soon all the normal social activities we had enjoyed together came to a complete halt.

We never went out to dinner any more, never took the children for walks in the park. We hardly ever talked; we kept a tight rein on our emotions. Our only conversations were about politics. Friends no longer came to the flat. I quickly lost touch.

It was around this time that I had a birthday, and according to our normal ritual for such occasions, Corin took me out for dinner. This was a rare treat. For about thirty minutes we sat in an uncomfortable silence. It was difficult for us to be alone now, for inevitably arguments would arise. Finally Corin broke the hush. "I should have remembered to bring the Communist Manifesto," my husband said. "We could have gone through it together, and I could have explained it to you, point by point."

It was not meant as a joke.

I looked around at the other people in the restaurant. They were talking animatedly, laughing, alive. I looked back at my stony-faced husband, horrified at our inability to communicate.

"Cor," I said, leaning across the table and grasping his hand, "I so want to be able to talk to you in the same way we used to talk."

He looked back at me with equal pain. I know he was as aware as I was of the gulf beginning to separate us, although I don't think either of us knew where it was coming from or where we were going.

"Times have changed," he replied. "There is work to be done now. Once we have made the revolution happen we can live a normal life again, be happy, but now is the time for struggle. I beg you to think about joining the Party, please join it with me. I love you and the children, but I'm totally committed to the Party and you will have to accept that fact in our lives."

I felt a chill in the room. I knew Corin well enough to know that this was no idle threat. I also knew he would always do what he felt was right. I didn't want to force him to choose between me and the Party. I thought I could probably coast with it for a while.

"If I forced you into a decision, or if you forced me, that would be blackmail," I said, "and all we will gain will be a dreadful hatred for each other."

He nodded. He knew. That night we went back to our flat, back to our children but not back to each other.

I tried to participate so as not to lose Corin altogether. Some nights later, we set off together for a meeting. We held hands as we walked up the street, but as we entered the house, Corin disengaged his hand from mine, as though embarrassed, and strode ahead of me. Even his posture changed. He became more upright, more aloof. The only acknowledgment of my presence now was a peremptory wave of his hand, indicating to me where I should seat myself. He had become another person before my eyes, his walk changed, his expression colder, his jaw rigid, his mouth set in a thin, tight line. He had an air of importance, of purpose, as he set about helping to organize the assembly.

Eventually we left, Corin once again reaching for my hand when we reached the street. Although I was discomfited by what I had seen, I was pleased that I had gone with him. It brought us a little closer, and I decided to keep my opinions to myself for the time being.

For Corin's sake I continued going to meetings and grew to know some of the members. I learned to my alarm that a broken marriage or a nervous collapse was an occupational hazard in the Party. The members worked so hard, for such long hours and with such ferocious intensity that often they burned out after a few years. The Party was known for having a quick turnover of members and a high incidence of broken marriages and other relationships. Only the really strong could survive the discipline.

I became aware of another displeasing fact. The young middle-class actresses who attended the meetings gazed at the Party orators in the same way that groupies gazed at pop stars. I would watch them as they fixed their wide eyes on one speaker after another, like hypnotized rabbits. It was quite a shock. The Party leaders had groupies. Corin had as many as if he were in a rock band. (Later I teased him, calling him "the lead singer of the WRP.") He was indeed magnetic as he stood there lecturing his audience eloquently and passionately on the need to achieve the dictatorship of the proletariat, bending the minds and hearts of his young followers to yet another regime, totally unaware of the devastating effect he was having on the women.

For us, a period of political invasion followed. Party meetings began to be held in our flat. As I was trying to cook the children their supper, people in anoraks would push past me, helping themselves to coffee. Corin would lift up the lid of the casserole I was attempting to put into the oven. "That smells good," he would comment, "but must you cook with wine? It's so expensive and bourgeois." The resentment built.

One evening, as I was sitting in the drawing room, enthralled by a television play, three complete strangers suddenly walked in and switched off the set. They began intensely discussing politics, never bothering to find out who I was. I was angry but I felt too intimidated by them to do or say anything.

Another time, during a miners' strike, a group of northern coal workers in London to picket the House of Commons stayed in our flat for days. They were polite and considerate. I cooked meals for them and made them feel at home. The day they were leaving, they thanked me politely, and then asked who I was.

They did not even know that Corin had a wife.

"I'm Deirdre Redgrave. I'm married to Corin," I said.

They were embarrassed. They looked at each other quickly. "Of course!" they said, and nodded. I knew that in their tightly knit families they would never subject their wives to similar humiliation.

A family crisis suddenly loomed large on the horizon. Jemma was asked by Michael and Rachel to present a bouquet to Princess Margaret, who was to attend the opening of the Redgrave Theater in Farnborough. The theater was originally to be called the "Michael Redgrave Theater," but Michael, with typical modesty, felt that as his offspring were now attracting an equal limelight, the name "Redgrave Theater" would be more appropriate.

Corin refused point-blank to allow Jemma to present the bouquet. As a member of the WRP, he felt he would look ridiculous in the British press if his daughter were seen curtsying to a member of the monarchy, an institution to which he was totally opposed. Jemma was disappointed; she desperately wanted to be allowed to attend the opening and meet the princess. Michael and Rachel thought Corin's attitude absurd, but it was up to him to make the decision. I could see his point of view but was tired of politics always coming before family needs.

At last I reached my limit.

Luke's sixth birthday dawned one bright Saturday morning in April. I arose early in order to make the cakes and jellies for the mass of children who were to arrive in the afternoon for his birthday party.

At about ten o'clock, the flat was suddenly invaded by fifty Party members who had arranged to meet there in order to rehearse a cabaret program they were performing to raise Party funds. Every room was filled with people, yelling and screaming.

Into the kitchen, wrapped in a bedspread, materialized our extremely neurotic Algerian au pair girl.

"Come with me quickly, Allah is in my room!" she cried. "He has told me I am pregnant with the New Messiah." Well, what could I say? I followed her, dumbfounded, into her bedroom. She knelt on the floor, raising her arms heavenward. "Look, look, there he is, can't you see him?" she cried hysterically.

I looked at the ceiling, and all I could see were strips of peeling paint.

"Look, look," she cried. "It's wonderful, he is saying the New Messiah will be born in this flat, everyone here has open minds."

Mine was closing rapidly. I fled to my bedroom only to be confronted by a voluptuous female member of the party, clad in next to nothing, doing a bump and grind to David Rose's famous music, "The Stripper." They had added political words, and it was now called "The Asset Stripper."

I noticed Luke watching goggle-eyed in the corner with a little giggling coterie of friends. The perfect birthday present! Even in Corin's study I found an actor dressed as Lenin rehearsing a rousing speech to the proletariat. Where was I? In a mosque? A nightclub? Russia in 1914? In the drawing room, what seemed like the massed choirs of England were singing the "Internationale" in full voice.

I thought I must be going mad. "Luke's birthday cake," I managed to remember, "I must ice Luke's birthday cake," and I returned, somewhat hysterically, to the kitchen.

The birthday party was, in the teeth of so much chaos, a great success, but exhausting. It was a great relief when Vanessa turned up in the evening with a present for Luke. It meant we could sit down and have a drink, and I could pour out my troubles to her. She was very sympathetic—in those days she had as little time for the WRP as I did.

Vanessa was not yet involved with Corin's politics and Gerry Healey's party, but she had become passionately involved with a stunning young English actor, Timothy Dalton, whom she had met while filming *Mary Queen of Scots*.

Corin was determined that she should follow him on the path to the party. Timothy, on the other hand, wanted her to remain with him, independent and free. Corin and Vee had had since childhood a very strong relationship, and Corin could be ruthlessly self-willed. Their battles were as tough as their love for each other, but not so enduring.

Corin's involvement with the party and Vanessa's with the hippie ethics of Timothy Dalton caused the beginning of their first serious rift. Corin would call her "John Birch" and try with debate, ridicule, and relentless pursuit to hook her into his new obsession.

But Vee was too much in love to be bothered by Corin's attacks, which to her seemed irrelevant. She was more concerned with going for long walks at Odiham in the freezing cold wearing shorts to ensure that her legs would not have that dreary post-winter pallor. She knew how she wanted to look when she arrived in Australia (there the height of summer) to meet Timothy, who was touring.

I sympathized. After all, I had been in love. But where was my lover now? Stuck in a dingy hole with a bunch of yelling Marxists, instead of wandering the countryside with me, picking the first bluebells and primroses of spring.

Inevitably, however, Corin's relentless will prevailed upon that of his sister.

Vee's relationship with Timothy hit a difficult patch. In her pain and confusion, she threw herself into a new cause. Corin and Gerry Healey provided a focus for all that foundering emotional energy. By the time her relationship with Timothy was once more on an even keel, she, like Corin, had been completely won over by the Party and was totally committed to it.

Timothy, like me, had never joined the Party. I felt a great deal of sympathy for him. I knew before he did what it feels like to have someone you love expend so much time and energy in another direction. It created great difficulties for them, but he has stood by Vanessa, although disagreeing with some of the stands she takes. They appeared together again in *Agatha;* he played her husband. He has played her husband on the screen twice, but not in real life. Real life would mean living with the Party, so although they still see each other constantly, and have had a close relationship for a good ten years, often spending holidays together with her children and mine, they have always maintained separate houses.

I know that he, like I, was hurt by how much of themselves Corin and Vanessa gave to the Party. But he, unlike I, was able to remain steadfast in his love, despite the fact that in the last decade the politics of the Party has become more important to Vanessa than anything else in her life.

I clearly remember Vanessa's saying long ago, when she and I would talk freely and openly of our feelings about everything from men to philosophy, "I have always loved fanatics. They are," she added seriously, "the only truly genuine people in the world."

Since then she has become one herself. Embracing extremist causes as radical as the Irish Republican Army and the Palestine Liberation Organization, she uses her power of oratory and her compelling presence to try to indoctrinate whoever crosses her path and to dismiss those who do not conform to her beliefs.

When she played Isadora in a film she became Isadora. When she played Fania Fenelon, she grimly scoured her skin with blunt razor blades to mark her face. When she played Lady from the Sea, she soaked herself from head to toe every night so she could walk onto the stage fully clothed and dripping wet. When she walks at the side of Yasir Arafat she wears the combat boots of the PLO and a Palestinian headdress. But I have come to feel that she was caught as much by the romance of the rebel, the idea of revolutionary heroism, as by a harsher reality.

In the meantime, my life was becoming increasingly difficult.

I was feeling so stifled at home that I determined to prove to myself and to Corin and the world that I was a woman in my own right.

It wasn't anything new in the media, but it was a big charge for me. The women's movement was making itself heard and felt. Women were getting new opportunities, new freedoms, equal rights, equal pay. I now wanted it for myself.

I started to work for the first time since I had had children. Jemma and Luke were now attending school all day so I was at last free to pursue other interests. A girlfriend and I started an antique clothes shop in an antiques market. The shimmering sequined dresses of the thirties and forties were becoming fashionable, as were the clinging printed crepe dresses with padded shoulders of the forties. We started to be successful, and for the first time since my marriage I was able to buy a package of cigarettes without asking Corin for the money.

Having again money I had earned myself changed my whole attitude toward myself. I hadn't realized that being dependent on Corin for money had made me feel dependent on him for too many other things as well.

At the age of twenty-four I had felt middle-aged. Now, at thirty-four, I was beginning to feel young. Just as Corin never realized how much I wanted my independence, he didn't realize how glad I was to be free of my imaginary debt. He didn't know because he really didn't care. I was past disgust with his lack of sensitivity; I was bored. When he left to film *Between the Wars* in Australia, I was actually relieved that he would be away for three months.

It was a crucial time for my burgeoning self-confidence.

Regaining the interest I had lost in my appearance, I bought new clothes and makeup and paid some attention to my hair. I took down the political posters that were lining our walls. I put up all my own favorites, early Presley and James Dean, in a gesture of defiance.

I had been bored for so long that I felt I had nothing interesting to say. Since the Party, Corin would only talk *at* me. I would sit before the fire I had just lit, cuddling a child I had just bathed, longing for peace. But the flames would flicker, the child's head would drop in sleep, and Corin's rhetoric would go on and on until he bored the very rafters off the ceiling.

I spent the three months Corin was away rekindling my interest in other people, and through that interest in my own self again. I relaxed, my children relaxed, we laughed.

One night I got home about four in the morning. I'd been to a concert, then gone on to a club with some of the friends I had rediscovered while he was away. I had danced the entire night and felt exhilarated.

My shoes creaked on the polished floorboards of the hall as I crept in, trying not to wake the children. As was now usual in our relationship, Corin kept his comings and goings deliberately mysterious. I hadn't known when he would return from Australia, but I was concerned not to disturb my sleeping household.

Unfortunately my shoes clattered to the floor. Corin was back, and he woke up, furious. My relaxed, waltzing mood was shattered.

I was "too late," I had been "acting in a ridiculous way," I had "woken Jemma." "What kind of mother are you?" was the final taunt. And then Jemma came sleepily out of her room rubbing her eyes, and said sweetly, "But, Dad, you've only just got home, too!"

"It is quite unfair of you, Corin," I said, mustering as much dignity as I could, "to accuse me of enjoying music when you enjoy politics so much."

Corin huffed back into our bedroom and shut the door, and I slept alone on the sofa.

With Corin home, our previous pattern of life was resumed with a vengeance. I had ceased to attend Party meetings, but the invasion of Corin's comrades into the flat continued. They were now openly aggressive toward me; they had finally realized that I was not about to follow Corin into the Party, and they attacked furiously in a constant verbal onslaught.

"Why don't you support Corin?" they would shout as I was trying to grate cheese for the cauliflower. "If you don't support us it means you're hostile to us. How can you be hostile to your husband? If you don't join us and start selling papers, you are betraying not only the Party but the entire working class."

I almost threw the cauliflower at them, sauce and all.

Earl Green, an actor who was staying with us and who was an old friend of mine, had witnessed many of their attacks on me and was shocked.

"If you were my wife, I'd go berserk listening to guys talking to you like that," he said.

Corin was sometimes witness to it, but he did not take a blind bit of notice, even when I was near tears. By now he was too immersed in his role as revolutionary hero to care. I almost believed he *would* shoot us if we impeded the revolution, as he had once shouted to me in anger. One day he gave me the biography of Lenin's wife to read. I was astounded at the man's ego. I remembered how often I had heard it said among members of the Party that Corin was to be the new Lenin.

Earl was a friend of Corin's as well as mine, and, intrigued by the whys and wherefores in the change that had come over him, wanted to see the Party in action for himself. One night the two of them set off to Equity's annual general meeting, where representatives of the Party were to make some proposals.

Earl arrived home alone and angry, infuriated at how the members of the WRP would cause valid issues about the rights of actors to degenerate into ridiculous arguments about the downfall of the Tory government or capitalism in general.

It surprised Earl that people had cheered a remark made by a non-Party member at the Equity meeting about "two members of our extreme left who had been held over their potties by uniformed nannies." He had had no idea how unpopular Corin and Vanessa had become. They antagonized people even within their own ranks. The anger they roused was extraordinary. Perfectly sane, balanced, upstanding citizens would suddenly become apoplectic when the name Redgrave was introduced. The daggers would strike: "How dare they go around creating trouble! They should stick to what they know best—playacting—and leave the rest to professional politicians." And again, as people had always said of Vee, "All they really want is publicity."

Of course, it was the last thing they wanted. It was the one thing they had always had and didn't need. But this bombardment from every side left me with no answers for myself or anyone else.

There seemed to be no escape from the barrage, not in religion, "the opium of the people," as Corin would taunt, not even in sleep. In the early morning, what had been a soft walk up and down the corridor when he woke at five in order to be at the factory gates to sell the WRP newspaper to the workers had suddenly become a stomp.

"If I have to get up at dawn, then so do you," the steps seemed to say.

I imagined Corin's mad legs tearing up and down the flat. I could hear them even with pillows over my head. I felt I was losing my mind.

Even as I was trying to shut out the sound of my husband's agitation, I was finally realizing I could no longer live with it. The momentous revelation quite terrified me. It meant I had to do something about my life, but I didn't know what, so I did everything I could to put off making a decision, to put off starting the process of separation.

I'd been living with Corin Redgrave for nearly ten years.

18

Reflections of the Soul

Had Corin been a compulsive gambler or an overt womanizer, it would have been easier to deal with than the fact that he was a politics junkie. There is no medication for it, and no antidote. In the face of his total commitment to his beliefs, I felt bewildered and inadequate.

My feelings of inadequacy became overwhelming. I was suffering from loss of husband and the safe structures of marriage. My own identity was slipping away from my shaky grasp again. This time it just about completely disappeared.

The only time I felt at peace, away from the demands of husband and children, was when I sat in the bath, locked away from worry, allowing the steaming water to drain away my tension.

Friends, common sense and a stiff drink had always solved almost anything, but nothing was working for me. I could not approach friends because I felt I was not the person they once knew. I felt like an autumn leaf, victim to the slightest breeze that could blow it in any direction.

I could not even turn to the Church. My faith had long ago been ridiculed to death.

In desperation I dialed the number of an eminent psychiatrist who was an old friend of Rachel's, and was relieved to notice in the telephone directory that she lived close by. Just getting out of the flat was becoming a problem, and I was glad I didn't have to struggle through dense London traffic to Harley Street, where most consultant physicians had their offices.

I decided to tell Corin of my plan. He didn't object; he could see me falling apart and didn't know what to do about it. The following morning, filled with apprehension, I duly set off to see the doctor.

But after a few appointments, instead of feeling reassured and more confident, I was actually feeling worse, as though my entire personality was fragmenting. The doctor's kind and soothing words did not help the state of high anxiety and depression I seemed trapped in. I wanted desperately to have something tangible to hold on to, and the children were my only touchstone.

The more confident Corin appeared in his role as the revolutionary, the more fragile I felt.

The crisis came one night.

"I'm shaking, Cor," I said, frightened, waking him. "I don't know what's happening. I can't stop shaking. It feels as though shock waves are sweeping my body from head to toe and I can't stop them. I don't know what to do."

Corin simply took me in his arms and very, very gently made love to me, the first time in months. He wordlessly understood my crucial need for reassurance and affection. He knew instinctively the only way to give it was through the body. By the act of physical communion we could somehow touch each other in a way we had not for a long time, and that would put me back in touch with my own strength.

But in the morning I knew I had to find someone else to help me. I knew I was out of control. I wanted medication and my doctor disapproved. I was shaking again. I made coffee for Corin, and as we sat across the kitchen table from each other I said, "Listen, Cor, I know I need to go to someone else for help, I need to get some pills, I can't go on like this. Look at my hands."

I stuck my fingers out in front of him and watched them tremble, mesmerized by my own inability to control the basic functions of my physical self.

Corin turned away. He finished his coffee. Rose from the table. Said merely, "I have to go out to a meeting now. You do what you think best."

He had left me again. The tenderness of the night before had dissipated in the light of day.

"But Corin," I pleaded, "I just can't go out on the street alone. I can't drive. It's not safe for me to drive. Please drive me to Harley Street. I'm really frightened."

But the cold look was back in his eyes. When he touched me briefly it was not as though he were really touching me. The Party had taken over again; I could feel the personality change. I had learned to recognize that insidious shift in loyalties, and when I felt it happening it frightened me almost as much as my own changes. But the Party came first.

I discovered another psychiatrist through an old friend of my parents', who put me straight onto medication to relieve my by now overwhelming anxieties. He forced me to recognize myself, to see myself as a woman with concrete choices to make, and make soon. It was the first time in a long while I had felt real.

When I read in the newspapers about women leaving their husbands, I wondered if they had ever felt as I did. Who were these brave creatures? They were the new breed of woman. They seemed to bear no relationship to me. I wondered if their relationship with their children was as intense as mine, or if perhaps I was hiding behind my children. I recalled the heroic exploits of my courageous ancestor, the brave Ursula Hamilton, of my namesake, the romantic Deirdre, Celtic Queen of Ireland, and felt feeble in comparison.

Joan, my closest friend, advised me to stop thinking about it; she said that one day I would wake up and know what to do, that all the conflicts in my conscious mind were being slowly resolved in the unconscious. It was a long and agonizing wait.

Throughout all the months of vacillating, Rachel became my

adviser and comforter. It was she who had put me in touch with the first doctor, the woman that she herself had turned to in times of crisis; it was Rachel who understood, more than anyone else could, what it was like being married into the Redgrave family. She willingly took the place of my mother, who was still living abroad. And though I wasn't her daughter, and I was inevitably going to hurt her son, Rachel could always reach across the gaps with warmth and understanding.

Almost every weekend I would take the children to the Odiham cottage. It was always to see Rachel. Michael was rarely there because he was working, and at weekends he often preferred the rather more sophisticated circle of his London friends.

I loved Rachel very much. When I felt lonely and abandoned she would carefully explain how in many ways the Redgraves were very selfish or self-motivated people. She encouraged me to leave Corin and search for my own identity because she knew well that ruthless streak in all of them, and knew it would not change, not for anything or anyone. She had lived through it too, and though she was proud, and practically never showed her hurt, I knew she had suffered too.

As I poured out my heart to Rachel over scrambled eggs and cups of tea late at night, I found myself apologizing. "I know Corin is your son," I would say to her. "I don't want to erect a barrier between you and him. But you have to know what's going on. I simply cannot stand all those people in the Party invading my home and taking my husband away. All the socialist principles in the world can't stop a child's crying at night because he's missing a father and can't stop a woman from feeling cold because the space in the bed beside her is empty."

Rachel knew what I meant.

"Deirdre, please always feel I'm your friend," she said. "We have both married into a family of extremely brilliant people who will always put themselves first. Or their causes. You are young enough to make your own life. I am no longer able to strike out for myself. We are fortunate to have known them, to know them, but it does not always make for an easy life."

Years ago Rachel had decided to endure it. She felt that on balance it was worth the heartaches. I knew I could not.

During our talks she revealed how she felt she had taken that decision, and abandoned, for several crucial years in her youth, a potentially dynamic career because her own mother had been so very selfish, completely dominating her beloved father. Rachel was determined since childhood not to allow the same pattern to permeate her life. So she veered to the other extreme, giving in to Michael about everything, from educating the children to tossing an omelet. In his turn, Michael always depended on her utterly as the mainstay of the family. She was and is the backbone of his life, and now that his health is so bad, she has even returned to the stage and television, working constantly to maintain their standard of living.

As much as she loved my children, they in turn gave all their childish love and trust to her. Rachel represented to all of us— children without anchors—a warm center of gravity. Whatever changes took place within her volatile family, she stood fast.

Rachel is still a fine-looking woman. Very like Vanessa, but softer and much smaller, her expression more humane perhaps.

We sat across the kitchen table from each other and I thought how sad and beautiful her face was. "Take your chance," she said. "I understand you must. Now *you* have to understand that." At that moment I loved her dearly. Although I had found her somewhat stiff toward me, or perhaps absent-minded, when I first married Corin, I knew now that I was fortunate to have such a rare and honest woman as my mother-in-law.

I realized that Corin and Vanessa's move to the absolute fanaticism of the WRP had made her a victim as much as it had me. Every time Corin or Vanessa moved stridently into the BBC or the National Theater, taking one or the other over for a program of shouting their slogans, Rachel's contemporaries in the legitimate theater would descend on her, objecting violently to her children's actions.

"Oh, God, Rachel," people such as John Clements, Laurence Olivier or Marius Goring would say, "what on earth are your children doing? They're making absolute raving idiots of themselves!"

Rachel, of course, would defend them to the death, although the displays of her two eldest embarrassed her. Like me, she was quite able to comprehend Corin and Vanessa's original theories, but could not condone the way in which they set about implementing them. Rachel's way of dealing with her children was to keep an open house for them and as much of an open mind as she realistically could. Michael sidestepped the controversy because he was simply hardly ever at home.

Lynn's way of dealing with her brother and sister's fanaticism was to depart lock, stock and barrel to America forever. They had often asked her to speak at their fund-raising affairs. But she would have nothing to do with their politics at all. She still loved them as people, but has often reiterated on talk shows and in the press that she is completely opposed to their stand and wishes to lead her life only as actress, wife and mother.

The weekends at Odiham gave me some sense of peace. That Corin's mother could support me in my decision to leave her son gave me an inner strength. Although by the time we got back to London and all its madness some of the tranquillity of the countryside had dissipated, I know that I could not have gone through those months without Rachel's stoic presence.

19

Fleeing the Cage

Corin had no inkling of the depths of my disorientation. It was obvious from the brusque way he treated me that he had no sympathy. Instead of wondering why I never combed my hair, went out, saw friends, cooked meals, he simply accepted my behavior with a touch of irritation. He succeeded, as usual, in making me feel like a wayward schoolchild who would eventually come around with patience and a little more discipline.

I began to hate his smugness. The worst thing was that he would not react. However I acted, however I looked, I could see no reflection of who I was or what I was doing from him. He would just look at me without expression and walk away.

Then one day he told me he was leaving "on Party business" for a few weeks.

"Perhaps some time on your own will help," he said coolly, not with sympathy, but with ill-concealed contempt.

I was glad to see him go. He had already been away too long for me to miss him now. The door closed without him saying goodbye.

In the weeks he was away, Corin never once telephoned, even to ask after the children. I was disgusted, but it reinforced my understanding that it was I who was responsible for these children, that I mustn't look to Corin for a parental support he could clearly no longer give. That knowledge helped to strengthen my wavering resolve to strike out on my own.

Also, while he was gone, I found I could function normally again. I actually felt better. I hadn't gone so far as to wear makeup or go out dancing, but at least when I looked in the mirror the image bore some resemblance to an attractive woman.

Corin came back one morning as I was standing at the sink doing the dishes. He looked at me vaguely and inquired where I'd put some Marxist tract he was looking for.

I stared at him blankly. He had been away for weeks and he didn't even say hello. "Oh, yes, Corin," I said bitterly. *"The First Five Years of the Communist International*, by Trotsky. My bedtime reading. It's under my pillow and the bedroom's the second on the left."

Corin glanced at me, turned on his heel, and left the room.

I shot after him, just in time to see the door close softly in my face.

Corin and I had reached the end. One of us was going to have to put a stop to all this pain. That the someone was going to be me was now clear. As soon as I had made that decision the hurt began to recede. I made an appointment for that afternoon with one of the top divorce lawyers in London.

The autumn day wrapped a beautiful red-and-gold mantle over the city. I felt warm and wonderful, proud of myself for making a decision at last. I took a bus for part of the way and then hopped off when it got to Green Park and began to walk through the same grass that Corin and I had trod when we were first engaged. It suddenly came upon me as I shuffled through the snapping leaves that this was me coming full circle. This park was the one Corin and I had run through, hand in hand, just before our marriage, when we were deciding to make our lives together for eternity.

Now I felt numb. Not running—trudging. I was going to a

lawyer, going to destroy completely that ephemeral dream Corin and I had built all those years ago. To make sure I was awake I kept curling and uncurling my fingers inside my coat pocket.

I stood in the impressive waiting room until a smartly dressed man introduced himself and showed me into his office. The moment had come. I sat, frozen in my chair, looking around me. The office was expensively furnished and paneled in mahogany. On the large desk in front of me I noticed the picture of a pretty young woman, obviously the lawyer's wife. "Some people make a go of it," I thought as tears of sentimentality mixed with self-pity began to trickle down my cheeks.

"Don't you worry, my dear," the lawyer said cheerfully. "We'll hit him for every penny."

"I don't understand you," I muttered.

"Don't you worry," he repeated. "By the time we've finished with him, he won't have anything, I understand you have two young children. Judges are very sympathetic to cases like yours."

I could see that the man had no idea of Corin's and my true financial situation. People automatically assume, because you have a famous name, that you have money.

"I'm sorry," I said. "I don't think we understand each other. I have come here to find out my situation with regard to custody of the children, should I decide to leave my husband. I don't want to 'hit him' for anything. I just want to be clear as to where I stand according to the law."

He was a man whose clientele clearly consisted of rich women who had been abandoned by their husbands, and like hell's furies were determined to make them suffer for it. He began to ask me details of my sex life and whether or not Corin beat me.

I felt I was talking to someone from a different planet.

When I arrived home, Corin was making tea in the kitchen. He welcomed me lovingly, his change of mood, as ever, unexpected. "Sit down in the drawing room—I've lit the fire. You look so tired."

My home felt loving and warm, the atmosphere so different

from that I had just encountered in the lawyer's office. Once the children had had their tea and gone to play in the garden, I told Corin the truth.

"I have been to see a lawyer about getting a divorce," I said, the words echoing back to me as if someone else had said them.

Corin went white. "Dee, do we really have to do this?"

"Yes," I said. I turned away. I could not look at him.

"But we love each other," he said.

"I know, but you know as well as I do that the situation is hopeless." I ran into his arms and we hugged each other, each lost in private despair. Corin could not give up the Party. I could not live with it.

At last Corin had to face the hard reality of my disenchantment. It was a total shock to him. He had grown so used to my tolerance, my ability to maintain the family, that he had mistaken it for subjugation. I don't think he ever seriously considered the possibility that I would leave him. When he had it slammed up against him like a cold blade, it was a death for him. He was knocked completely off balance. It took me hours that night to talk him into any kind of understanding of my point of view.

He could never bear to lose at anything. To lose at marriage humiliated him.

"But you *can't* leave me, Dee," he said. It was almost an order.

"But I have to," I replied. "Don't you see what's happened to us? It's not just that I can't believe in the same things you do any more—and that's crucial enough in a relationship—but half the time I don't even know what you're talking about. I don't like the people you bring into our home. They don't acknowledge me, they don't talk to our children, whose home it is, too. *You* don't talk to our children!"

"But what's going to happen to them now?" he asked, predictably. "They don't want me to leave. I'm their father. They would be heartbroken if we separated."

"But have you any idea how many weeks and months you've spent away from them? And then, when you weren't working and you could have spent more time with us, the Party meetings came first? And when you'd go off to one of your meetings rather than help your son with his homework?"

I was beside myself. I couldn't help it. All the hurt and anger unspoken in these last years came boiling up to the surface. Tears were streaming down my face. This was the part that hurt the most.

"Other friends taught them to swim!" I shouted. "Other people taught them to play chess and ride their bicycles. Where were you when those things were happening? What are your daughter's favorite books? Did you know she needed a new pair of jeans? Do you ever think of taking us all out to dinner once in a while? Do you ever think about how bloody *lonely* I get?"

Corin was flabbergasted. He just stood motionless in the middle of the room.

"Every year since I can remember you've said you were going to take us all on holiday. First of all, the promise was a whole two weeks. I've never seen it last longer than a long weekend, and it's never been anywhere more exotic than a friend's weekend cottage. You were needed so badly by the Party. The *Party!*" I was practically spitting by this time. "And then you had the cold, bloody nerve to say that when it came right down to it, you would *kill* us for the sake of the revolution!"

Corin tried to make a move toward me. He tried a rational approach.

"Now listen, Dee." His voice dropped an octave and he fiddled with his glasses. "You of all people understand why I do what I do. We have discussed it many times. You know what the world needs and what I am supposed to do about it."

I was furious. How dare he make me a conspirator in his game?

"The Party means nothing to me," I said. "Whatever you think you're doing, as the new Lenin, or Healey's successor, I don't want to see you doing it. If that's what you want to do more than be my husband and the children's father, then go ahead and do it but don't involve me. I've had it."

For days the arguments continued. "You *won't* regret it if you stay with me," Corin would say. "Have more children with me," he would urge.

"But you don't even see the ones you have!" I would cry in despair.

So finally, slowly, we came to an agreement.

"We should spend some time apart," said Corin one day. "The Party has asked me to do some work in Scotland. I could go up there for three months."

"That would give us each some time to think," I agreed.

I could think of no better answer. I needed time. I did not want to run into the streets with my children on either arm. Running my clothing shop did not bring in much money. I had no clear vision of the future, apart from my desire to discover for myself who I really was as a woman.

I knew Corin thought he was just giving me time to come to my senses. I saw it as a key being handed to me that might or might not unlock the door to a new life.

For days after Corin left I basked in a sense of space. It was not just that there was no Corin, no nagging, no arguments— there was no Party either. No more boots tramping through my home or insults hurled through my kitchen. No more telephone calls breaking into the night as Corin's comrades called him to arms without so much as saying, "Hello, how are you, sorry it's the middle of the night."

There was time to spend with children and girlfriends. Time just to think, to read, to walk to the cemetery down the road, my favorite place of quiet spirits. The children seemed free of tension. I was glad to see them laughing carelessly again. The constant bickering and sometimes outright furious rows had taken their toll.

The word that Corin had left for a while soon circulated among my old friends. Knowing they didn't have to run the gamut of

Corin's interrogation every time they came to my flat, they began to visit me unexpectedly, and soon our home was ringing with music and conversation again. It was fun to have fun. Just what I needed to lift the gloom of the last months.

Trisha asked me to a party and I said yes gladly. I knew the people would be young and interesting, the food excellent and the music new. Stimulation was just what I needed.

I dressed for the evening carefully, choosing soft silks and beautiful embroidery from my collection of antique clothing. I loved clothes that were rare and exquisite. Usually I sold them to other people, but just a few I kept for myself, and on this occasion I wanted to look glamorous, seductive, frothy, a fair creature of luxury.

Jemma came into the room as I was pinning my unruly hair into a chignon. Already I found the children more possessive of me. Since Corin's absence they always asked me where I was going, who with, and whether they could come too.

"Not this time, darling," I told my pretty little daughter. "I'm going to a party tonight and I'll probably be really late. It's for grownups and you wouldn't enjoy yourself at all."

I wasn't sure how she would react to this news. She and I had already had a couple of mother-daughter run-ins. She was a delightful child, but at nine was just beginning to step into that confusing area of prepubescence, never quite sure if her mother was protector or rival.

But tonight she seemed enchanted by the woman she saw. "You look beautiful, Mum," she said with awe, and met my eyes shyly in the mirror. My throat caught and I bent down swiftly to hug her. It had been a long, long time since I had felt truly beautiful. But tonight, I knew, she was right.

The party began in the early evening. I planned to move on later to a club where I knew my favorite old blues singer, B. B. King, was playing.

I was tense as I arrived. But as I moved through the flower-laden room, lit by candles, full of music and chatter, I realized there were many people there I knew. There was no need for me to feel afraid. I felt the sweat of nervousness dry on my skin. My body relaxed. I talked to my friends, and I sounded quite normal.

Mickey Lumley and Jonathan Benson were there and we talked and talked. It was not until several hours into the party that I was introduced to Speedy Keen. He was Island Records' golden boy, the singer in whom they were currently investing vast amounts of time and money. He had just signed a deal with Chris Blackwell, which meant he would be leaving his first label, The Who's Track Records, and leaving the management of my old friends Kit Lambert and Chris Stamp, who had made their names in the rock world by discovering The Who.

Speedy's band, Thunderclap Newman, had had a hit single with a hauntingly lovely song called "Something in the Air," which reached the tops of the charts worldwide and later came to be regarded as one of the classic rock anthems of the sixties.

I liked Speedy instantly. He made me laugh. He looked at me so hard I thought he could see right through me. A long-nosed, long-haired funky East End kid making it good, he had a kind of no-holds-barred honesty that appealed to me.

When I woke up the next morning I found that what I most remembered about the party was Speedy Keen's face. And the cockney voice with the lilt of laughter in it, and the hook nose and the penetrating eyes and the humorous curve to the crazy mouth.

I hadn't thought about a man with such warmth for a long time.

I turned on the radio as I drove to work and admitted to myself as I was parking that I was waiting to hear if they would play something by Thunderclap Newman. Lost in memory of the night before, I was late in arriving to open the shop.

I'd been fumbling around in the old lace for quite a while trying to sort out what needed cleaning, what I should try to mend, and how best to arrange the next display, when suddenly I realized there was a tall figure standing over me.

"Hi!" said Speedy Keen laconically. "Want to come to lunch?"

My stomach rumbled as if in agreement. There was a little restaurant at the end of the antiques market. We could eat there. No harm in that. I agreed.

"You married then, are you?" was the first thing he asked, mouth full of sausage and mash. "Trisha told me you'd been married for a long time, to some actor geezer. Where's your old man then?"

I burst out laughing. "It's your subtle approach I like so much," I said to him. "What else would you like to know about my private life?"

"Everything," he said bluntly.

"You'll be lucky," I countered. But I did tell him a bit about Corin and me and he thought it sounded "daft" for a man to spend more time with a political party than his own wife. So did I. It all seemed very remote, all the ranting and raving and dogma and lonely nights. As though I were telling a story about two other people, not about me and my husband.

That afternoon we just talked a lot. Then he started coming around in the evening before going to the studio to record. Sometimes he would turn up very late at night, when recording session or rehearsals had finished. I began to look forward to these nocturnal visits.

And I was not at all sure what I was going to do about it. He grew more and more persistent in his pursuit. I was more and more tempted. I had been starved for the nourishment that comes with a good relationship for so long that my soul felt like a skeleton and my body craved reassurance.

"You've been deprived for a long time," he said quietly one evening, holding me, enfolding me. He kissed my lips. Corin, I remembered with bitterness, had not kissed my lips for more years than I could count. I succumbed.

We began a long, intense relationship that helped me surface from the loneliest struggle in the world, from an isolation terrifying beyond description. To look back into that abyss frightened me. Speedy was right. I had been deprived of a feeling of safety and warmth for a long time.

Speedy showed me my own beauty. He made me feel sensual again, and I was relieved that my sexual feelings had not withered along with my love for Corin. I did not yet understand fully that it is not enough to tie oneself to a man and let him lead. Later I would find that I needed my own answers, that I could be alone. That there would be other men, other loves.

20

Final Curtain

When Corin returned from his trip to Scotland just before Christmas 1974, it was to find life at home drastically changed.

I made decisions; I made money. With a blossoming career and a newfound confidence, I must have seemed like a new woman to Corin.

For the first few days he was home we circled each other warily, like fighting terriers about to pounce, fearful of the consequences. I wanted to protect the children from any ensuing battles.

We were sleeping together but not making love. It wasn't difficult to keep Corin at arm's length because it was clear we both felt more comfortable that way. In the mornings we had breakfast together before he went off to meetings and I went to the shop, Antiquarius.

A couple of times we tried to face each other. But already the dividing lines had been drawn. He had gone away too often. I had hoped that when Corin came back from Scotland he would want to move out completely. I thought he might finally face the fact, as I had, that we were living behind a facade. And our home was not a calm place in which to raise our children.

But he moved right back in as though nothing had happened. I suppose, for him, it hadn't. For him this past break was just another stretch of time. For me it marked the end of a marriage.

Finally I summoned my courage. He was standing at the kitchen table swallowing tea quickly before going off to sell the Party paper, *Newsline*, at the gates of a factory in West London. He had the teacup in one hand and a daily newspaper in the other, a neat way to avoid me.

"We have to talk, Corin," I said. He looked up from the paper for a moment, fixing me with those cold blue eyes. I wondered how long ago it was, and how wonderful it must have been, when they looked at me warmly.

I shook my head free of the thought. I wanted to raise the issue at hand before the children came charging in to grab their breakfast on their way to school.

"While you were away I decided I like being alone," I said. "I actually want to be alone. We never talk to each other or touch each other or even really look at each other now. I think you should move out."

"There's somebody else isn't there, Dee?" He asked me quite gently.

I had expected accusations. The beaten look that came over him took me by surprise. In the moments of sorrowful silence that sprang between us like someone holding a mirror to our past, I moved to touch him. The paper fell rustling to the table, and his arm came around me quick and hard as it used to in the early days of our marriage when he would touch me often.

He looked so sad.

"Cor," I said carefully, "it's true, I have met someone. But I don't want to live with anyone except the children. I need the space to work out the next step, and I can't work it out while we're still living together. It seems like too much of a sham to me. It makes me feel trapped and uncomfortable. I know now that the Party means more to you than anything else and I've just about come to terms with that. It's taken a long time and it's hurt me terribly."

For a period of adjustment, I felt he should leave the flat and move to St. Peter's Square to Vee's house in Chiswick. She was living there alone; Franco had long since returned to Italy. Timothy was there some of the time, but for the most part she was alone with her children. It was the obvious place for Corin to stay. The crusading Vanessa could shelter her brother. It might bring her down to earth a bit to take care of a cause so close to her heart.

Corin agreed. It seemed less like leaving home somehow. The house wasn't very far away, and we could see each other often. He could see the children, have them to stay with him if he wanted. The separation wouldn't wrench us apart, just gently reorganize our lives.

For the children's sake we would spend Christmas together. "I'll stay until Boxing Day and then I'll go," promised Corin. We decided simply to tell them that Corin would be away again for a while, since they were used to that. Telling them was not such a difficult scene as we had both imagined. Luke took it in his stride. The news worried Jemma more. She had felt the tension between us. She wanted to know where he would be and when he would be back.

"I don't know exactly, Jem," said Corin, hugging her. "But we'll have a wonderful Christmas. Let's worry about where we're going to find a turkey big enough for all of us first!"

A turkey—she could relate to that. We went on with preparations for Christmas, keeping as closely as we could to family traditions.

On Christmas Eve Jemma pinned me down. I was kissing both children goodnight. Suddenly her little arms came up and held tight around my neck so I couldn't move. "Where's Daddy going, Mum?" she whispered. "Will he be away for a long time?"

"Dad's going to stay with Vanessa for six months," I told her, swallowing a deep breath and taking the plunge. "Vanessa and he have a lot of work to do together for the Party, and I don't think I can live with the Party any longer. If they're living together under the same roof it will be much easier for everyone."

"Will he be coming back?" she asked directly.

"I don't know, my darling," I replied. "I simply don't know."

Jemma was aware of the family's dilemma. She had grown to hate the Party members as they invaded every corner of our privacy. She spent a great deal of time with her cousins, Vanessa's daughters Natasha and Joelly, who was born within three days of her and with whom she had a very close friendship.

I had often seen the little girls sitting around talking about how much they hated the Party.

"All those scruffy people marching around our house as though it was their home and not mine," Joelly would say, exasperated. And I would hear my own daughter answer her with stories of being booted out of her own bedroom.

"They come in and plot," hissed Jemma. "They don't care what any of us is doing. They just turn off the television if I'm watching something. They're horrible to Mum. And they just treat me as if I wasn't even there. I hate grownups who behave like that!"

Nevertheless she did absolutely adore her father. She was much too young to understand his politics, or why he could not or would not stop this invasion of her home.

Boxing Day was gray. Leaden. Corin and I moved in silence. We had breakfast with the children. I clasped and unclasped my cup of tea as though seeking warmth through the china from the hot liquid. I found I was still holding the cup in my hand when I went into our bedroom to get dressed. Corin was packing. I couldn't watch him pack. I went out.

We didn't speak again. There was nothing left to say. Our brave attempt to make this seem a normal parting in front of the children was belied by the absolute whiteness of his skin. I looked at his familiar face and saw it drained of color. Even his eyes looked pale, a kind of deadness behind them. I felt paralyzed. We didn't even touch or say goodbye. I stood in the doorway and watched as he walked away. I saw this suddenly frail figure moving away from me down the corridor. I saw hunched shoulders, a narrow back, a bent head. It was all I could do to stop myself from running after him.

During the period of adjustment that followed my separation from Corin, I remained close to Vanessa's children. Our adult alienation was never allowed to interfere with the tightly knit family relationships we had built up between the nieces and nephews over the years. All the children were very close. To allow our own difficulties to intrude on our children's love for each other was out of the question.

Joelly would come and stay with us for long periods of time. When Vanessa was away performing *Lady from the Sea* in New York, she sent Joelly to me for about three months.

Vanessa and Corin became more of a political team than ever. They were the fund-raisers and attention-getters of the Party. Corin would petition sympathetic people in the arts who had money, such as Jane Fonda. Vee would bring her politics onto the set of whatever movie she was making. The fact that they used people is part of what makes people so antagonistic toward the Redgraves.

Vanessa fanatically blended her career and her politics. She caused endless resentment among the crew when she was working on a film and would turn up at the gates of the studio every morning trying to sell handfuls of Party newspapers.

The publicity that she and Corin were receiving upset the rest of their family terribly. And now a full-blown scandal erupted, "The Red House incident," stirring the whole family into a turmoil, especially the children. *The Observer*, one of the most respected of London newspapers, carried a story that Corin (Jemma and Luke's *father*, Natasha and Joelly's *uncle*) was reported to be having an affair with actress Irene Gorst, who claimed that while visiting the Party headquarters at their "Red House" in Derbyshire, she was accused of being a spy for the

Special Branch and was subjected to hours of intensive questioning against her will. *The Observer* also made reference to arms caches hidden on the grounds.

The publication of the article touched off a storm of controversy which my marriage could not survive. After the article appeared the police raided the "Red House" looking for weapons.

Corin's response to the article and raid was typical; he claimed that it was a setup, that the police and *The Observer* had worked together to frame the Party. Since he and Vanessa were prime media targets, he said, anything could be manipulated to sound like a horror story. He and Vanessa and others named in the story sued *The Observer* for libel.

All I could do was reassure the children and tell them that there was some misunderstanding. Then, when Corin asked me to go to court with him, I faced the most difficult decision in our marriage. I knew that he needed my support in the eyes of the world: if he was such a monster, would his estranged wife be sitting there beside him every day? It was, in a sense, my final act as a Redgrave.

As it turned out, Vanessa and Corin and the others did not recover any damages and had to pay out nearly 75,000 pounds in legal costs. But in spite of this, they still claimed they had won because of the nature of the verdict. Corin claimed victory because the jury had found that parts of this article were indeed defamatory and were not substantially true. *The Observer* claimed victory because the jury also found that those parts that had not been proved to be true were so inconsequential as not to damage the Redgraves' reputation.

Corin was confused and furious at the verdict. He, typically and immediately, mobilized all resources and organized a benefit concert at the Lyceum to raise the money.

He even involved his mother, who, although not a left winger, had always exhibited public loyalty to her headstrong children, whatever personal misgivings she may have had. This time she was prepared to lend her considerable presence to their fundraising attempts. "I can't have my children being branded as dangerous bullies, and I won't," she told me. "So I just do whatever I can to help."

Michael would not have anything to do with the fund-raising. He did not believe in bringing politics into art or into family relationships. He was also suffering terribly by now from Parkinson's disease, which eventually and tragically rendered him incapable of pursuing his career.

In the event, Corin and Vanessa's night at the Lyceum was quite spectacular. Black singer Madeleine Bell sang her heart out. Rachel read poetry while Corin played the piano. Vanessa descended from the ceiling to the stage, like an Amazon priestess. She was swathed in her costume for the film *Bear Island*, which she had just been shooting in the Antarctic; the effect was dramatic. Her entrance was engineered to look as though she'd just flown in by helicopter.

I looked at the three striking Redgraves, the first time that all of them had ever been on stage together, their height, the magnificent bone structure and blazing eyes, and their unmistakable voices ringing with passion and seduction.

But I knew it was only staged—a staged performance by stage actors. When the final curtain fell to wild applause, Vanessa again emerged and began her harangue to the people.

"Thank you for supporting us. Thank you for being here. We must all defend ourselves from fascist attacks of this nature," she cried. "The right wing press is against us. We must counterattack. We cannot let such things happen, it's prejudice of the worst, most dangerous kind!"

She ranted on and on and on. I was so tired of it all. It was growing more and more bizarre to me that this famous movie star who had just flown in from earning vast amounts of money, making an expensive film in an exotic place that most people cannot even fathom they will ever see, could dare to entreat a crowd of ordinary working people to give her money, for whatever her cause.

"Why on earth should she *expect* them to part with their money?" I muttered angrily to my companion. But my question fell on deaf ears. Vanessa is persuasive. People are moved by her impassioned speeches. Only I seemed to know the script.

When I saw my friend who was on the dole and hadn't been able to find a job in eight months donate a pound, I left the theater. All the passion, all the flair, had become irritating melodrama to me.

The Redgraves were products of their own and other people's illusions, but I was no longer under the Redgrave spell.

As I walked out of that tumultuous theater into the calming night rain, I realized that I had had enough of theater, and enough of theatrics. Only I and my children were real.

I had married into one of the most illustrious, talented, pig-headed, idealistic and controversial of all acting families, the thorny flowers of England's acting aristocracy. I played out my own private drama among a handful of powerful actors, each of whom, in a unique way, is able to bend the ear and alter the vision of the beholder.

The Redgraves are a remarkable family. I once wanted more than anything to become part of it; for a while I was enchanted. This was a stage in my life. They were the players.

ABOUT THE AUTHORS

Deirdre Hamilton-Hill Redgrave has been a model, run an antique-clothing shop, and designed clothes for commercials and film. She was married to Corin Redgrave for fourteen years. Now she lives in London with her son Luke and her daughter Jemima.

Danaë Brook is a journalist contributing to, among others, the Los Angeles *Weekly* and *Rolling Stone*, and, in London, the *Daily Express*, the *Daily Mail*, the *Observer*, the *Sunday Times*, the *Sunday Mirror*, and *Sun Day* colour supplement. She is the author of *Naturebirth*, a book on preparing for natural childbirth. Ms. Brook lives with her husband and three sons in London.